Curt Daniel's book *Basic Christian Doctrines* is an absolutely necessary primer in biblical teaching for church members. It has fifty chapters moving all the way from God's existence, His act of creation, and His acts of self-revelation to the final consummation of history in Heaven and Hell. Each chapter, averaging around four pages each, has ten assertions about the respective doctrines and then simple Bible-centered explanations of each assertion. Curt's style is enviable for its simplicity and straightforward confidence and clarity. The simplicity only makes it easy to read, not lacking in profundity. It is slim in words, not skimpy on the rich biblical, historical, theological, and polemical context out of which these clear affirmations arise. In places where Bible-believing, Reformed, evangelical Baptists disagree, Curt gives a brief recognition of the difference and, where possible, suggests some kind of synthesis for slightly differing viewpoints. He never allows such engagements, however, to deflect from the profound message that the Bible is a revelation—clear, meant to be understood, designed to give strong convictions about things unknowable apart from revelation, setting forth a true knowledge of man and God and His redemptive purpose, with transforming power, and given that we might know that Jesus is the Christ and eternal life is found in His name.

– Tom J. Nettles

There are a good number of systematic theologies in print—weighty tomes needful for the church. But there is also a place for smaller overviews of the Christian faith, less complex but equally profound. This sketch of the key tenets of the Christian faith fits this bill perfectly: both concise and solid. A great resource for those interested in the Christian faith, new Christians, and older believers who need to revisit the basics!

– Michael A.G. Haykin,
FRHistS Chair and Professor of Church History,
Director of The Andrew Fuller Center for Baptist Studies,
The Southern Baptist Theological Seminary, Louisville, KY

This handy resource you hold in your hand by Dr. Curt Daniel accomplishes nearly the impossible—it provides very succinct yet incredibly accessible definitions of fifty basic doctrines on the Christian life. Usually, other attempts to accomplish a work like this fall flat. Either the subjects are treated with far too much verbiage—thus unnecessarily lengthening the prose, or else easy enough to read but are much too elementary in content. Daniel, however, deftly succeeds with both aims where many other writers do not. With an astounding economy of words, he explains biblical truth with great clarity. These are just some of the things which make this small volume extremely valuable for personal or group study. Our many thanks to Free Grace Press for giving the body of Christ such a needed and helpful book!

– Dr. Lance Quinn
Executive Vice-President,
The Expositors Seminary, Jupiter, FL

BASIC CHRISTIAN DOCTRINES

BASIC CHRISTIAN DOCTRINES

CURT DANIEL

FGP
FREE GRACE PRESS

FREE GRACE PRESS
CONWAY, ARKANSAS

Basic Christian Doctrines

Published by

Free Grace Press
3900 Dave Ward Dr., Ste. 1900
Conway, AR 72034
(501) 214-9663
email: support@freegracepress.com
website: www.freegracepress.com

Printed in the United States of America

Cover design by Scott Schaller

ISBN: 978-1-952599-45-3

For additional Reformed Baptist titles, please email us for a free list or see our website at the above address.

Contents

Foreword

About four years ago, I acquired an early manuscript of *Basic Christian Doctrines* by Curt Daniel, and I was amazed by the ingenious simplicity with which he is able to summarize Christian doctrine in such a modest, manageable, and understandable format. His treatment is thorough without being overwhelming, careful without being pedantic, and easy without being superficial. I found myself turning to the manuscript frequently when looking for ways to summarize and explain difficult truths.

Shortly afterward, I was asked to teach an extensive overview of systematic theology to a group of church leaders overseas in a concentrated course. I decided to let Dr. Daniel's manuscript serve as our textbook, and it was the perfect resource.

When I learned Dr. Daniel was preparing the manuscript for publication, I was delighted. Christians everywhere—new believers as well as seasoned saints—will find this work useful and edifying.

Despite its brevity, the work is rich with helpful Scripture references and insightful explanations of hard concepts. Dr. Daniel always seems to find a way to illuminate difficult matters without belaboring fine points. Whether you are doing independent study or assembling a course syllabus, you will find his outlines and analyses immensely beneficial.

I should note that there are a few points of doctrine where I would see things differently from Dr. Daniel. (I take a different view than he does, for example, on the order of end-times events.) But these are rare and never fundamental differences. Even when you disagree with him, you will find Dr. Daniel's insights profitable and thought-provoking. His tone is delightfully charitable, though his convictions are never ambiguous. It's a refreshing and highly readable style.

In an era when doctrinal understanding is on the decline and reliable helps for serious-minded Christians are increasingly hard to come by, *Basic Christian Doctrines* is a welcome volume, filling a niche that has been vacant for a long time. I hope it remains available for years to come.

Phil Johnson

Director, Grace to You

Preface

Not long after my conversion while in college, I read two books by the late Paul Little. They were poignantly entitled *Know What You Believe* and *Know Why You Believe.* I got the point and agreed wholeheartedly. I still do. Christians still need to know what and why they believe. They always will.

Unfortunately, the importance of doctrine is downplayed in many quarters. As David Wells has shown in his excellent *No Place for Truth*, many Christians have capitulated to postmodernist notions of truth. They echo the relativist mantra, "It doesn't matter what you believe as long as you are sincere." But according to the Bible, such a view is not only erroneous, it is dangerous. It makes all the difference in the world what one believes about God, man, ethics, the hereafter, and a host of other subjects.

Fortunately, God has provided us the truth we need. It is found in the Bible. Trite as it may sound to skeptical ears, "The Bible tells me so" is an extremely profound and relevant truth with powerful implications. The little book you hold in your hands is simply an effort to organize the Bible's teachings on the major topics it contains.

This is not meant for the scholar but for the average Christian. The chapters were originally prepared as weekly handouts for a class I taught at Faith Bible Church in Springfield, Illinois. As such, it can be used by Sunday school classes or Bible study groups. The fifty chapters can be covered in a year. It can be of special help to young men considering seminary education and pastors who have not had access to formal seminary training.

I make no claim to being original. I offer no radical insights that pretend to revolutionize the world of theology. I do not engage in detailed dialogues or point-for-point refutations of other viewpoints. I present very few quotations or illustrations and only the occasional reference to the original Greek or Hebrew words. My aim is to be concise yet extensive. I cannot say everything, but I can say something.

Each of the fifty chapters contains ten basic statements followed by a paragraph of explanation and appropriate biblical proofs. There is naturally some overlap of material. The late John Gerstner frequently organized his theological lectures around ten points with the explanation, "After all, the Lord Himself summarized His own Law in Ten Commandments."

This little handbook may also serve as a bridge between two other useful tools. First, the great creeds, confessions, and catechisms of the past have stood the test of time and are more valuable than many contemporary Christians realize. My own favorite is the 1689 Baptist Confession of Faith (also known as the Second London Confession), which is the Baptist revision of the classic Westminster Confession of Faith. Second, it may encourage the reader to read much larger systematic theologies and other books on specific topics. A brief bibliography is found at the end.

Let me openly state my theological perspective and methodology at the outset. It is Christian, not non-Christian; Protestant, not Roman Catholic; evangelical, not liberal; Calvinistic, not Arminian; Baptist, not paedobaptist; practical, not theoretical; dogmatic, not speculative; and biblical, not philosophical.

I usually quote from the New King James Version (NKJV) of the Bible but occasionally have used my own translation.

I wish to thank the members of Faith Bible Church for receiving this material as first presented, Mrs. Christa Morgan for preparing the original handouts for publication, Mrs. Elizabeth Smith for her expert editing, and my good friend Phil Johnson for his encouragement and assistance in bringing it to fruition. All errors, however, are my own.

May the Lord bless readers with grace and light as they study the infallible Word of God with this small work.

1

Introduction to Christian Doctrine

1. Doctrine is important.

The Bible places a high value on doctrine. For example, God often says, "I want you to know" (1 Cor. 11:3; Col. 2:1). God gave us the Bible so that we might know certain important things (1 John 5:13). Sadly, too many Christians know very little about the Bible and Christian doctrine. They often know more about sports than about God's Word.

2. *Doctrine* means teaching.

In the Greek New Testament, there are two words for *doctrine*: *didache* and *didaskalia*. Both mean teaching, instruction, education, and explanation. Proverbs 4:1–2 equates doctrine with "instruction" and "understanding." A doctrine is a statement about a specific truth. It is a statement, not a command or a question. Jesus taught doctrine (Matt. 7:28; 22:33; Mark 1:22; 4:2; 11:18; 12:38; Luke 4:32, etc.). One of the main characteristics of early New Testament Christians was that they followed "the apostles' doctrine" (Acts 2:42).

3. Doctrine must be true and sound.

God says, "I give you good doctrine" (Prov. 4:2). Acts 13:12 (KJV) calls it "the doctrine of the Lord." True doctrine must come from God, not from mere men. Even the Lord Jesus said, "My doctrine is not Mine, but His who sent Me" (John 7:16). Paul placed a very high value on doctrine which is true and sound (1 Tim. 1:3, 10; 4:6, 13, 16; 5:17; 6:1, 3; 2 Tim. 1:3; 3:10, 16; 4:2–3; Titus 1:9; 2:1, 7, 10). And 2 John 1:9–10 says that we are to ignore any so-called Christian who believes or teaches anything other than "the doctrine of Christ."

4. Sound doctrine is an anchor against the danger of false doctrine.

You can't fight something with nothing. We need true doctrine to fight and be defended against false doctrine. False doctrine is not only useless, it is dangerous. Ephesians 4:14 warns us against the winds of false doctrine. Hebrews 13:9 says, "Do not be carried about with various and strange doctrines." Jesus warned of "the doctrine of Balaam" and "the doctrine of the Nicolaitans" (Rev. 2:14–15; cf. 24); "the doctrines of men" (Matt. 15:9; Mark 7:7; Col. 2:22); and "the doctrines of demons" (1 Tim. 4:1). Truth sets us free (John 8:32). God urges us to note and avoid those who cause divisions "contrary to the doctrine which you learned" (Rom. 16:17).

5. There is no substitute for a good knowledge of Bible doctrine.

God desires to feed us His Word and we become spiritually malnourished when we do not graze in the pastures of His Word. We become imbalanced, anemic, confused, easily led astray, prone to doubt, and backslidden. Some Christians do not recognize the hunger pangs they are suffering when they are not studying the Bible. Doctrine alone does not produce spiritual maturity, but there is no maturity without it (Heb. 5:12–14). It is erroneous to say, "I just want Christ, not doctrine." Christology is the doctrine of Christ (2 John 1:9–10). Nor is it true that "doctrine divides." False doctrine divides; truth unites.

6. A disciple is a student.

The New Testament regularly uses the word *mathetes* to describe the followers of Jesus. The word means disciple, student, learner. To be a good student, one must be teachable (Luke 11:1). He must admit that he does not know certain things (see 1 Cor. 8:2). This is a school from which nobody ever finally graduates, for there is always so much more to learn. God wants us to learn enough so that we can teach others, who in turn will teach others (2 Tim. 2:2). We should be able to teach our children (Eph. 6:4) and new converts and answer the objections of unbelievers (2 Tim. 3:16–17). But some Christians have not learned enough to be teachers, though they have been saved more than long enough. They need to be students again (Heb. 5:12). A student should strive to become a teacher (Matt. 10:24–25).

7. All Christians should know what they believe.

A new Christian naturally hungers to be taught, like a new baby hungers and thirsts for milk (1 Peter 2:2). Too many Christians outgrow this desire and think they know enough. All Christians, not just preachers and theologians, should know Bible doctrine. Ignorance is no virtue. God often says, "I do not want you to be ignorant" (Rom. 1:13; 11:25; 1 Cor. 1:8; 1 Thess. 4:13; see also 2 Peter 3:8). Willful ignorance is sin (2 Peter 3:5). There are no acceptable excuses, such as "I'm too busy," "I'm not a great intellectual," or "It's not that important." Every Christian can and should have a strategic grasp of the Bible and basic Christian doctrine.

8. God gave us minds and expects us to use them.

A mind is a terrible thing to waste. God created us with minds as well as bodies, and commands us to use both to His glory (Rom. 12:1–2). The first and greatest of all God's commandments is "You shall love the LORD your God with all your heart, with all your soul, and with all your mind" (Matt. 22:37). It is ingratitude, laziness, and selfishness to use our minds in such a way that we neglect learning what God really wants us to know. He also gives Christians "the mind of Christ"—the indwelling Holy Spirit so that we can spiritually learn (1 Cor. 2:16; see also Eph. 1:18). It is dangerous mysticism that tells us to turn our minds off and go by our feelings (see 1 Cor. 14:15).

9. God gave us teachers to teach us the Bible.

Jesus Himself was a teacher, a rabbi, a theologian (John 13:13). God has given many lesser teachers as gifts to His church in order to teach and instruct us (Eph. 4:11). The word for teachers is *didaskalos*, related to the word for doctrine. A teacher teaches doctrine; he is a doctor of doctrine. We are to learn from those teachers which God has given to us and ignore "false teachers" who teach contrary to the Bible (2 Peter 2:1). Teachers are not as important as what they teach. God gave us a Book of words to learn and teach, not a book of pictures to look at. Teachers are to teach the Bible (2 Tim. 4:2).

10. Doctrine must precede practice.

Doctrine and practice are important, but they must be in the proper order. They also must not be separated. Doctrine without practice is dry, stale, and useless, producing only pride. Practice without a valid doctrinal foundation can be legalistic or mystical. The more we know, the better we can live for God. The indicative statements precede the imperative commands. We must be willing to learn and obey (John 7:17). And the more good Bible doctrine we know, the more our faith grows and the better we can love and worship God.

2

Theology

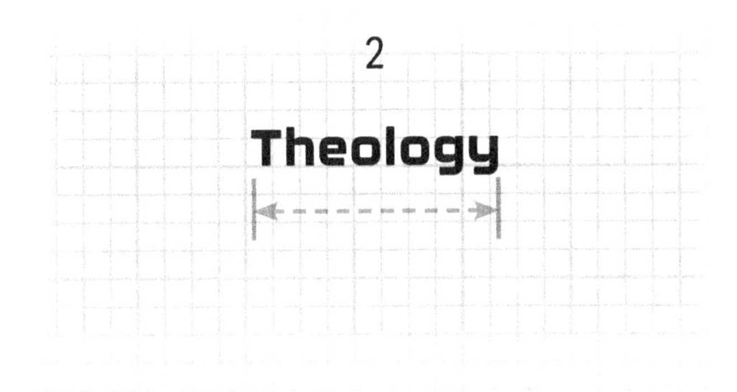

1. Theology is the science of God.

The word *theology* comes from two Greek words: *Theos* (God) and *logos* (word, idea, study, science). Theology is the science or study of God, just as biology is the science of life, anthropology is the science of mankind, and zoology is the science of animals. Theology was once commonly called "divinity," meaning the science of divine subjects. Theology is concerned with God, His Word, and His works. True theology is based on the Word of God (2 Tim. 3:15–17). Theology, then, is simply serious Bible study.

2. Biblical theology is the theology of individual parts of the Bible.

The term *biblical theology* refers specifically to the study of the individual books and authors of the Bible. It is based on *exegetical theology*—the study of individual words and sentences. Each book has a distinctive contribution to the Bible and can usually be summed up in single sentences (e.g., Mark 1:1; John 20:31; Romans 1:17). Even the four Gospels, which overlap in much of what they say, have distinctive emphases (Jesus is King of the Jews, Messiah, Son of Man, and Son of God). All these are links in the great Bible chain. All complement each other; there are no contradictions. Biblical theology is also concerned with the chronological progression and development of God's revelation and work in history, culminating in Jesus Christ (Heb. 1:1–2).

3. Systematic theology is the organization of Bible doctrines into categories.

Systematic theology deals with the Bible as a complete entity. Just as a deck of cards can be dealt out numerically, it can also be categorized by suits. The "whole counsel of God" (Acts 20:27) concerns the entire message of the Bible and is more concerned with God as the one author than with the individual human authors. Serious study of Scripture shows that certain topics are repeated and developed. For example, Jesus engaged in systematic theology in Luke 24:27 when he took the apostles through the Bible on the theme of the Messiah and His work. The Bible contains a system of truth, sometimes called "that form of doctrine" (Rom. 6:17) or "the pattern of sound words" (2 Tim. 1:13). This explains the harmony of all the parts and shows the many interrelationships of individual doctrines. God is a God of order (1 Cor. 14:33, 40), and so is His Word. Among the categories are *Christology* (science of Christ), *soteriology* (salvation), and so forth.

4. Historical theology is the development of theology in church history.

Just as biblical theology deals with the progression of revelation in history, so historical theology deals with the progression of the study of revelation among Christians. But the two are not equal in importance. Church history deals with Christians, events, dates, places, churches, and the like. Historical theology deals with the theological controversies, theologians, books, councils, and so on. Few heresies are really new. Truth and error have debated repeatedly on many fronts. Certain truths were discussed and challenged at specific times in particular: the one true God (up to AD 200), the person of Christ and the Trinity (200–400), justification by faith (1500–1600), etc. Similarly, each Christian engages in his own personal historical theology as he grows in the study of the Bible.

5. Practical theology is the application of theology to Christian living.

Practical theology shows the relationship between biblical principles to personal practices. It explains the underlying reasons behind biblical commands and examples. Thus, there is a theology of evangelism, prayer, church life, and many others.

6. Tradition is oral teaching.

Tradition can be good or bad. The word *paradosis* is used in a good sense in 2 Thessalonians 2:15 and 3:6. The prophets and apostles and even our Lord Jesus spoke many things not written down in Scripture (John 20:30; 21:25). However, we have no authoritative record of those teachings. The Jews had the idea that Moses orally passed on divine revelation to the elders, who in turn orally passed it down to those in the time of Jesus. But Christ rebuked their placing tradition on the same level as Scripture (Matt. 15:1–9). This Jewish tradition was later written down as the *Mishnah*. The Catholic Church repeated the same mistake. Oral tradition may be useful for a short time, but it easily becomes rumor, opinions, and the traditions of men, in contrast to the commandments of God (Col. 2:8, 22). Tradition, therefore, is not a solid foundation for theology. Only the Bible is.

7. Religion is the practical theology of worship of the God/gods we believe in.

The word *religion* can be good or bad. James 1:26–27 uses both concepts. The good sense is that Christianity is the true religion. It alone provides the true way of worshiping God. All other religions are false. But religion, or the practical exercise of worship, must be based on theology and not the other way around. Christianity is more than rituals and ceremonies. Moreover, the elaborate Old Testament worship ceremonies were replaced with two simple ceremonies (baptism and Communion), and now the emphasis is more spiritual. True religion is neither magic nor superstition but the worship of God in Spirit and in truth (John 4:24).

8. True theological method is important.

Both the content and method of theology are important. There is a right way to do theology and many wrong ways (such as basing it on tradition, philosophy, etc.). True theology must be based on the Bible alone; that is the basic principle of theological method. True theology presupposes the total truth of the Bible. Theology is received by revelation of God, not conceived by the mind of man (Col. 2:8; 1 Cor. 2:13). God is the subject, not merely the object, of theology. That is, He Himself teaches us about Himself. Thus, there are both similarities and differences between theological and natural science. We do not study God like we study an amoeba under a microscope. Another important principle is seeing how the New Testament uses the Old Testament. The Bible itself uses logic, but logic itself must be subject to the Word of God, else it becomes mere philosophy.

9. Some theological truths are explicitly stated in Scripture.

The most important truths are explicitly stated, such as "God is love" (1 John 4:8, 16); "God is light" (1 John 1:5); "In the beginning God created the Heavens and the earth" (Gen. 1:1); "The Lord our God, the Lord is one" (Deut. 6:4); and so on. Some are given only once; others, many times. They are universal and absolute, undeniable, and irrefutable (1 Tim. 3:16; Luke 1:4). They are plainly stated, yet infinitely profound. They are like axioms, maxims, and formulas.

10. Other theological truths are logically derived from Scripture.

By comparing spiritual truths with other spiritual truths (1 Cor. 2:13), we derive other great theological truths. The word *Trinity* is not stated in any one verse of the Bible, but the Trinity is the implicit teaching of Scripture, seen when we combine verses such as Deuteronomy 6:4 and Matthew 28:19. The New Testament sometimes draws on underlying principles of certain Old Testament verses and develops a new doctrine or practice (e.g., 1 Tim. 5:17–18). Thus, principles of theology are important. But we must be careful to observe the limits of this theological method and stay close to Scripture and avoid speculation.

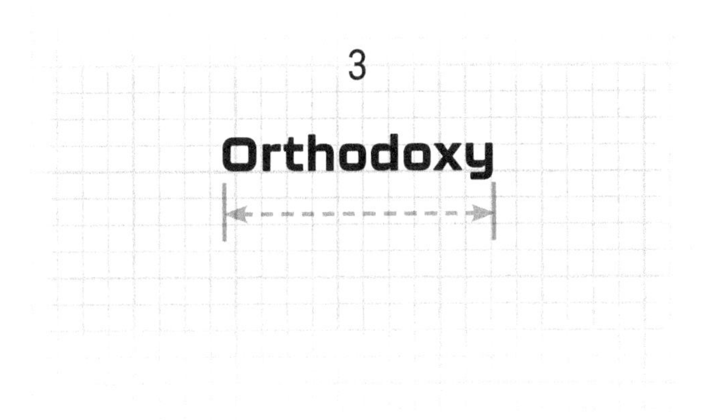

1. Orthodoxy is right doctrine.

The word *orthodoxy* comes from two Greek words meaning "right doctrine." It is not used in the New Testament, but the idea is the same as "sound doctrine" in 1 Timothy 1:10, 2 Timothy 4:3, and Titus 1:9 and 2:1. We use it in English to refer to the right mainstream as opposed to the unusual fringe (such as orthodox medicine vs. alternative medicine). The Greek Orthodox Church once held to biblical orthodoxy but no longer do. The test of Christian orthodoxy is not antiquity but Scripture. That doctrine alone is orthodox, which is biblical. In turn, orthodoxy must produce *orthopraxy*, or right practice.

2. Some truths are essential and foundational to all others.

All Bible truths are true, but some are "of first importance" (1 Cor. 15:3–4). Hebrews 6:1 calls them "the elementary principles of Christ." They are the basics, the ABC doctrines. In theology, we call this *dogma*. Dogmatic theology is concerned with the essential truths of Christianity. *Dogmatic* doesn't mean stubborn or obscurantist; it means firm commitment to truth. Christian dogma is not defined by a church (as Roman Catholicism claims for itself), but by the Bible alone. One must believe these essential truths to be a real Christian. It is impossible for someone who rejects, substitutes, or adds to these essential truths to be a true Christian. These are *sine qua non*, or "that without which," Christianity is not Christianity. It is dangerously wrong to say, "It doesn't matter what you believe as long as you are sincere."

3. The gospel is the main message of the Bible.

Among the essential doctrines is the gospel. *Euangelion* means "good news" or "good message" (Mark 1:15; Luke 2:10). It is a divine record of facts to be believed, not a command (that is law). Specifically, 1 Corinthians 15:3–4 sums up the gospel as the truth about the person and work of Christ: the God-man who died for our sins and rose again. There is only one true gospel, but many false gospels (Gal. 1:8–9). The Old Testament preached the same gospel in advance by prophecy (Gal. 3:8; Luke 24:25–27, 46–47). The true gospel calls for only one response for salvation: faith and repentance (Mark 1:15; Acts 20:21). To add good works or baptism to this is to preach a false gospel. To preach the gospel is simply to present the basic truths about Jesus Christ.

4. Evangelicalism and fundamentalism are two kinds of orthodoxy.

Evangelicalism and fundamentalism are differently described by scholars, but in general they differ mainly in how they relate to theological error. Evangelicals defend the gospel, but some (sometimes called neo-evangelicals) seem to emphasize peace and unity over a strong stand for the truth of the gospel. Fundamentalists are always aggressive in defending the gospel. Both believe the same gospel and defend it from non-Christian objections. Both terms have been subject to misunderstanding and misuse, and some people suggest they have lost meaning and should be abandoned. A key verse is Psalm 11:3, "If the foundations are destroyed, what can the righteous do?" We need to believe and defend the fundamentals of the faith (Jude 3).

5. Orthodoxy is also called "the faith."

Another term for this basic content of Bible Christianity is "the faith" (1 Tim. 1:19; 3:13; 4:1; 5:8; 6:10, 21; etc.). It refers to those basic doctrines that are to be believed. Saving faith has a content, known as the faith. Jude 3 calls upon us not only to believe it but to earnestly defend it. The "analogy of faith" (see also Rom. 12:6) means that we study the Bible with reference to this basic message. Any interpretation that contradicts the basic gospel is automatically a wrong interpretation. We need to see the harmony of the entire Bible's message, structured around this basic theme of orthodoxy, the gospel, and the faith.

6. Heresy is false doctrine.

Orthodoxy is true doctrine. Heterodoxy is false doctrine. The technical word here is *heresy*, meaning one's own views that divide from others. In practice, it produces wrong schisms. In general, all error is wrong. But in a more precise sense, heresy means the rejection of a fundamental truth. One can still be saved if he is in error on a secondary truth but still believes the essential truths. But rejection of any of the basics is heresy and theological poison. Scripture repeatedly warns against promoters of heresy as false prophets (Matt. 7:15), false teachers (2 Peter 2:1), and false brethren (2 Cor. 11:26). God pronounces a curse on those who preach a false gospel (Gal. 1:8–9). Heresy is no small thing. It attacks the very essentials of the faith. Those who believe heresy do not believe in the fundamentals and are not true Christians. Heresy primarily refers to pseudo-Christianity, not non-Christianity.

7. Apostasy occurs when a person no longer professes orthodoxy.

Apostasy is not the same as backsliding. True Christians backslide, but they do not lose their salvation. Apostasy occurs when someone who once professed the truth of the faith now rejects it. This is what Hebrews 6 discusses. Judas is a good example. Apostasy is spiritual and theological treason. There are degrees of apostasy. One may reject only one essential doctrine but still profess the others, such as when someone goes from evangelicalism to Roman Catholicism, Mormonism, or other brands of pseudo-Christianity. Full-blown apostasy is when someone who once professed all the basic truths now rejects all of them, such as when one becomes an atheist. There will be a great apostasy one day, as predicted by 2 Thessalonians 2:3 and 1 Timothy 4:1.

8. A creed is a short summary of what you believe.

After the time of the New Testament, early believers were challenged by the Romans and other pagans: "What do you believe?" The Christians replied by producing short summaries of the faith. The word *creed* comes from the Latin word *credo*, which means "I believe." A creed, then, is a short summary of the faith or orthodox fundamentals. Some passages in the New Testament hint at the idea (1 Tim. 3:16). The earliest creed is known as the Apostles' Creed (second century), but was not composed by any of the apostles. It meant that this is a summary of the gospel preached by the apostles. The Nicene Creed (early fourth century) amplifies it in order to emphasize the deity of Christ. The Apostles' Creed is popular with Protestants, the Nicene with Catholics. A third early creed is the Athanasian Creed, based on the teachings of Athanasius in the fourth century. It mainly deals with the Trinity. A Christian ought to be able to summarize his own creed.

9. A confession of faith is a longer summary of Christian doctrine.

Later, Christians expanded their brief summaries to include other doctrines. Some concentrate on specific truths which were debated at that time. Some are more theological, others more practical or ecclesiastical. If a creed is concerned with the primary doctrines of the faith, a confession of faith expands it to include the secondary doctrines. Most churches have a confession of faith. The best and most well-known ones are the Westminster Confession of Faith, the 1689 Baptist Confession of Faith, the Belgic Confession, and the Thirty-nine Articles. Many contain Scripture proofs.

10. A catechism is a confession of faith in question-and-answer form.

Catechisms were written mainly to instruct children and new converts. They are very useful for memorizing. The best ones are the Westminster Shorter Catechism, the Heidelberg Catechism, and Keach's Catechism (the Baptist version of the Westminster Shorter Catechism). Creeds, confessions, and catechisms are useful tools to study the faith. But they must be tested by the Bible, for Scripture alone gives us true orthodoxy.

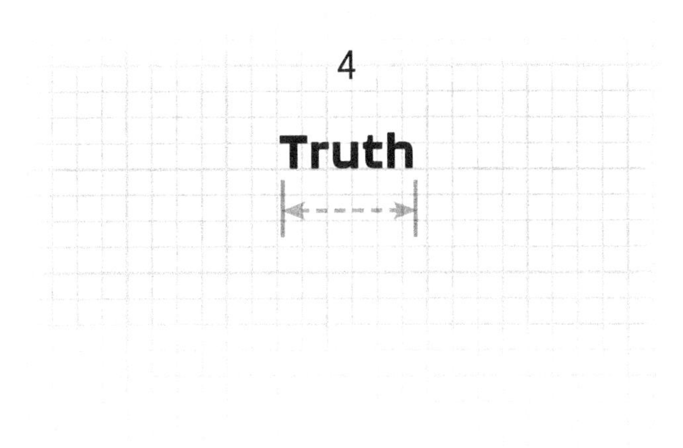

1. God is truth.

Truth is an important doctrine found throughout the Bible and is basic to the study of other doctrines. But truth is not an impersonal concept or idea. God is the final and ultimate truth. He is truth itself. He is the "God of truth" (Ps. 31:5). He is "the true God" (Jer. 10:10). The Greek philosophers asked three main questions: what is justice, what is beauty, and what is truth. Pilate asked, "What is truth?" (John 18:38). Jesus Himself is the incarnation of truth, for He said, "I am . . . the truth" (John 14:6). Truth is in Jesus (Eph. 4:21). God is the source of all truth, facts, existence, reality, and law. All real truth is God's truth. God is truth, speaks truth, defines truth. Someone said that God is the truth, the Bible is the truth about the truth, and fundamentalism is the truth about the truth about the truth. The Bible is the "word of truth" (Eph. 1:13) because it is God's word.

2. There is no such thing as a brute fact.

Cornelius Van Til popularized the theological statement that there is no such thing as a brute fact. He was right. No "fact" just simply exists in and of itself. All facts are true because God made them so. Whatever is true finds its source in God. For example, one plus one equals two. Why? Not because, "Well, it just does, that's all." No. One plus one equals two because God made it like that. God is higher than all facts. Even the laws of mathematics exist because of God. God does not say something because it is true; it is true because God says so. Facts are but little glimmerings of what God makes true.

3. Truth is not determined by man.

Since God alone is truth, truth is not determined by man, for man is not God. Truth is not determined by human vote, opinion, observation, science, or feeling. It is our job to discover truth, not invent it. Man has personal tastes and opinions, but these are merely subjective feelings. Humanism would make man the measure of all truth. This is but to deify man and dethrone God. How then does man discover truth? By receiving it from God. God reveals truth partly through nature and primarily through Scripture. Man's part is to believe it on the basis of God's authority.

4. Wisdom is seeing things as God sees them.

The first step is faith. We must believe whatever God says, otherwise we are calling God a liar (1 John 5:10). To believe God is to submit our minds to Him (2 Cor. 10:5). It is to recognize that God is truth and He alone has the right perspective on His creation. This is a truly awesome thing to do. "The fear of the LORD is the beginning of wisdom" (Ps. 111:10). Because we are finite and sinful, we do not see things as they really are. We need God to teach us. God's Word makes us truly wise (Ps. 119). The opposite of this wisdom is what the Bible calls folly—foolishness, insanity, nonsense. Sin is the very epitome of folly. It is spiritual insanity to believe one's own faulty perspective rather than God's.

5. Discernment is the ability to distinguish between truth and error.

One key aspect of wisdom is *discernment*. It is the ability to tell truth from error and good from evil (Heb. 5:14). Adam and Eve lacked it when they believed Satan and themselves rather than God. We need God's Word to be able to distinguish things that differ.

6. Truth and error are different.

Truth and error are opposites. They are irreconcilable enemies. They are as different as light and darkness. God is truth and light; in Him is no darkness or error (1 John 1:5). Among other things, this means that a statement can be true or false, but not both (see John 14:2). A statement cannot be true and false at the same time in the same way. We call this the *law of noncontradiction*, where A cannot be the same as non-A. God has made things the way they are and does not play tricks with us. It is not true to say, "The exception proves the rule" (exceptions disprove the rule and show that the rule was faulty). God is not a God of contradiction but of order (1 Cor. 14:33). The Bible has no contradictions. It is Satan, not God, that is the father of error and lies (John 8:44). Modern man greatly errs when he fails to see this difference.

7. Truth is reality.

The fundamental definition of the word *truth* is reality. A true statement is one that corresponds with reality. If we say, "The sentence, 'The dog is white,' is true," we mean that the dog really is white. The Greek word is *aletheia*. The Hebrew word is *emet*, which also has the implication of trustworthiness or reliability. Truth makes sense. Error is *non*-sense. Truth is real. The so-called Christian Science cult denies all this by saying that "all is illusion." No, God has created things as real.

It is sin that makes them illusions. We need to see things as they really are.

8. Truth is absolute, not relative.

Post-modern humanism teaches that truth is relative and each person invents his own truth. This is wrong, dangerous, and sinful. It simply is not true that "You make your own truth." We are created, not creators. We cannot create reality. To say that we can is to say that we are gods, which is what the Father of Lies wants us to believe (Gen. 3:5). Truth is absolute, not of itself, but because it is rooted in God. God is the final absolute and He does not change. The angels laugh and weep at the utter folly and nonsense of modern humanism's philosophical error that says, "That's your truth. Mine is different." Until all this is seen from God's perspective, we are lost in a jungle of man-centered, sin-dominated, blind insanity.

9. Truth is sometimes a paradox.

Truth is not contradictory to itself, but to error. Nevertheless, we are finite and do not generally see all the relationships between the things God has said and made. God has revealed some things as paradoxes. A *paradox* is an enigma, like "He that loses his life shall find it, and he that would save his life shall lose it" (see Mark 8:35). An *antinomy* is an apparent contradiction, or two statements which are equally true but we can't resolve how both can be true. For example, divine sovereignty and human responsibility are both revealed truths, but we do not fully grasp how they are both true. There are also mysteries, or things partly revealed and partly hidden (see Deut. 29:29). The Trinity is the mystery of mysteries. We know there is only one God and that He is three persons. But we cannot fathom the depths of this great mystery.

10. Profundity lies in simplicity.

One final thing about truth is important. The deepest theological truths are not the complicated ones, but the basic ones. A famous theologian once said that the most profound truth he ever learned was, "Jesus loves me, this I know, for the Bible tells me so." Often the deepest and most profound truths are stated in only a few words, like "God is love" or "Christ died for our sins." So, truth is to be received with childlike faith, which has a kind of naïve innocence to it. This is to be truly wise.

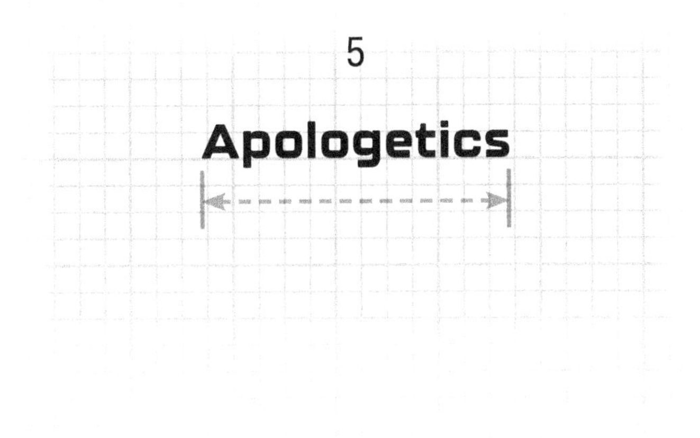

5

Apologetics

1. Apologetics is the defense of Christianity against non-Christian attacks.

God not only wants every Christian to know what he believes, but why he believes it. All believers must be able to give a good answer for their faith and hope (1 Peter 3:15). We call this *apologetics*, not in the sense of a wimpy apology for something wrong but a virile defense of something right. Every Christian, not just preachers and theologians, ought to be able to give basic answers to the objections and questions of unbelievers. It is especially useful in evangelism. If we don't know how to defend the gospel, we'll lose every battle. We need to refute those who oppose us (Titus 1:9). Apologetics specifically refers to answering the objections thrown at us by those persons and systems which do not claim to be Christian.

2. Polemics is the defense of Christianity against pseudo-Christian attacks.

Polemics is sometimes used of a more specific area of apologetics. It aims to refute and expose the various kinds of false Christianity. Our fight is not only with those outside the faith but with those who promote false gospels and heresy of the first order while still claiming to be Christian (Gal. 1:8–9). One is outright war; the other is sabotage and treason. Both are dangerous. Too many Christians ignore this front of the battle for the sake of peace and unity. But pseudo-Christianity is more dangerous than outright non-Christianity. The Bible repeatedly warns against false prophets, false teachers, wolves in sheep's clothing, and such who creep into Bible-believing Christianity (2 Peter 2:1; Matt. 7:15). Jude 3 commands us to "contend earnestly for the faith which was once for all delivered to the saints." We are to be watchmen on the wall (Ezek. 33).

3. Philosophy is worldly wisdom.

The word *philosophy* means "love of wisdom," but it is not God's wisdom. It is mere human wisdom, which is really foolishness. Colossians 2:8 specifically condemns philosophy as the invention of man. It does not come from God nor from belief in Christ. It is also condemned in 1 Corinthians 1. Philosophy sprang from Greece. In Acts 17, Paul opposed the Stoic and Epicurean philosophers. Plato, Aristotle, and Socrates were among the major ancient Greek philosophers. In the modern era, there are Hegel, Marx, Kant, Hume, and many others. Philosophy emphasizes the use of human reason, the mind, and rationality. If unchecked, it tends to become atheistic.

4. All non-Christian religions are false.

Philosophy is not the only ancient enemy. There are dozens of non-Christian religions, mostly coming from the East. They emphasize the heart, not the mind. They tend to mysticism and pantheism. Some are closer to the truth than others, but they all lead to Hell (Matt. 7:13; John 10:8). Even post-biblical Judaism is a false religion, for it does not accept Jesus as the Messiah, denies the Trinity, asserts salvation by works, etc. The main false religions are Islam, Hinduism, Buddhism, Judaism, Taoism, Sikhism, Jainism, and the general category of Animism, or spirit-worship.

5. There are three main kinds of pseudo-Christianity.

The three main groups of false Christianity correspond to the three main groups of unbelieving Judaism at the time of Christ. Roman Catholicism is like Pharisaism—huge, works-salvation, tradition-bound, etc. Eastern Orthodoxy is much the same. The second is liberal Protestantism, similar to the Sadducees in their rejection of revelation, weak ethics, etc. Then there are the many cults, like the Jewish cults of the Essenes, Herodians, Zealots, and others, which are exclusivist and esoteric. The earliest form of pseudo-Christianity was Gnosticism, opposed in Colossians, 1 John, and elsewhere.

6. We must use spiritual weapons to defend the truth.

According to 2 Corinthians 10:4, the weapons of our warfare are spiritual, not carnal (worldly). We use God's armor, not man's (Eph. 6). You don't fight fire with fire but with water. We are not to use the world's devices against them, else we have already lost. We may not use force, violence, brainwashing, fleshly temptations, entertainment, or other such means. Honest questions deserve honest answers, as Francis Schaeffer used to say. We may not use *ad hominem* arguments (insults against persons), but we must be gentle and humble, however unwavering (2 Tim. 2:24–26).

7. Some weapons are useful but insufficient.

Other weapons are acceptable but insufficient. For example, some Christians argue from miracles, fulfilled prophecy, the endurance of the Bible and Christianity through centuries of persecution, the enormous popularity of Christianity, the many favorable words said about Jesus by important non-Christians, personal testimonies, logical proofs, empirical evidences, and other such arguments. These all have their place but are not our primary resources, for each can be challenged in one way or another by non-Christians. At best, such arguments can only get a stalemate, not a victory. Such is the approach of Christian Rationalism, evidentialism, and others.

8. The Bible alone is sufficient to defend Christianity.

The Word of God is our main weapon (Eph. 6:17). Jesus turned to it not as a last resort but as His primary weapon in opposing Satan (Matt. 4), and so must we in fighting Satan's assaults through non-Christian and pseudo-Christian religions and philosophies. Our opinions mean nothing. God's Word is sharp and powerful, for God Himself speaks through it (Heb. 4:12). We do not use it as a magical or superstitious talisman but rather by knowing and believing it and quoting and explaining it properly and appropriately in fielding the objections of unbelievers. Two key statements in this context are "That's not what God says" (pointing out the error of an objection) and "This is what God says" (à la "Thus says the Lord" or "It is written"). See Matthew 22:29.

9. The best defense is a good offense.

Any team or army will tell you that defense is good, but you also need offense to win. We must know what our opponent is saying, and then we compare it with what the Bible says on that point. Don't bother with lesser details; stay with the essentials. Indeed, challenge the underlying presuppositions of the argument. A *presupposition* is the underlying and often unconscious assumption of a system of thought. *Presuppositionalism* is the kind of Christian apologetics that uses the

Bible to refute the basic and erroneous assertions and assumptions of non-Christian objections. It has been popularized by Cornelius Van Til, John Frame, Greg Bahnsen, and others. We must know the enemy (2 Cor. 2:11) and the weaknesses and inconsistencies of non-Christian views. It can help to show where such views logically lead. But mainly we are to show where they contradict what God says. Quote Scripture whether the opponent believes in the Bible or not. It is also important to be as clear in your words as possible.

10. It is better to know more about Christianity than about non-Christianity.

We need not know all the details of a pagan religion or worldly philosophy to refute it. Some Christians seem to know more about non-Christian theories than true Christian theology. Leave the detailed study to the experts and theologians. It is sufficient to know the basics of an opponent's views (ask him to sum it up for you or tell you where he disagrees with the Bible). Our job is primarily to know the Bible, for it is sufficient to enable us to believe and defend the truth (2 Tim. 3:16–17).

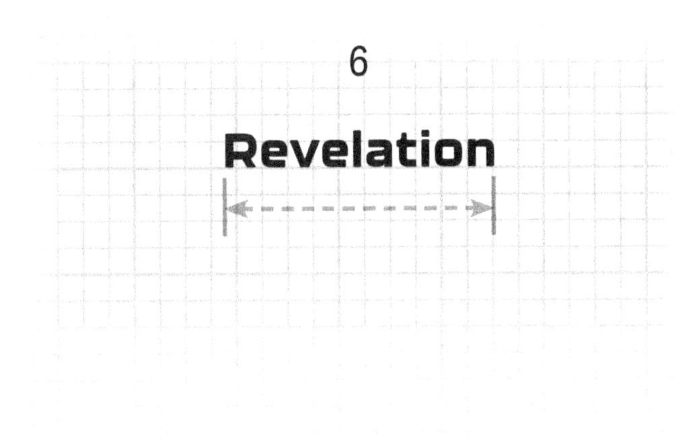

6
Revelation

1. God has revealed Himself.

God describes Himself as the hidden God (Isa. 45:15). He fills the whole universe but does not show Himself in His full manifestation except in Heaven. To us, He is invisible, inaudible, and intangible. He conceals Himself. But He also reveals Himself (Rom. 1:20). God is so great and far above us that we would know nothing at all about Him unless He chose to show us Himself—and He has chosen to do just that (1 Cor. 2:11–12). We come to know God only by God's initiative and revelation, not by our searching for Him by our own minds or efforts (Job 11:7).

2. God has revealed Himself only in part.

God has revealed some things about Himself and has left far more concealed. Deuteronomy 29:29 says, "The secret things belong to the LORD our God, but those things which are revealed belong to us and to our children forever, that we may do all the words of this law." What He reveals is true but not exhaustive. His revelation includes truths about the universe, man, sin, and especially about Himself. This revelation makes moral and ethical demands on us. Because only part is revealed, His revelation is often a paradox or a mystery, implying there is more to it than has been revealed. But it is never a lie or a contradiction. We may study His revelation, but may not pry into what is not revealed, such as the details of the future (Matt. 24:36; Acts 1:7; Dan. 12:8–9). It is God's glory to conceal these things and our responsibility to believe what He reveals (Prov. 25:2). We know only in part but will know far more when the revelation is full (1 Cor. 13:12).

3. God has revealed Himself gradually.

Hebrews 1:1–2 states that God has been revealing Himself in a variety of ways over the course of human history. We call this *progressive revelation*. God has been revealing Himself by stages and levels. Each one builds on the previous one. This is working up to a climax. God does this in actual history, not in mythological saga or make-believe, as many neo-orthodox liberals suggest. God also reveals Himself in various ways in different times and to different people. Similarly, when God sets out to save a person, He gradually gives him more light until he is saved, and then gives him progressive illumination and growth in knowledge.

4. God reveals some things by nature.

Psalm 19:1–4 says that the Heavens are God's handiwork that display His glory in a non-verbal way. Romans 1:18–20 adds that the creation tells us much about the Creator's attributes. We call this *natural* (or general) *revelation*. God reveals much about Himself in nature. For example, God's power is displayed in lightning, His holiness in the sun, His peace in a quiet lake, His truth in the laws of science, His wisdom in the design of man, His providence in the feeding of animals, His immensity in the vast number of stars, etc. All men everywhere have this revelation and therefore are without excuse. Moreover, God also reveals some of this through conscience, the echo of God's voice (Rom. 2:15). Yet God does not reveal His special grace and salvation through nature. All men know that God exists, but they do not know Him personally through nature.

5. God revealed some things by angels, dreams, and visions.

God spoke or showed things to select people by dreams when they were asleep and visions when they were awake. Sometimes they were transported "in the Spirit" to Heaven, in or out of their bodies (Rev. 1:10; 2 Cor. 12:1–4). These were not natural dreams like we have today but supernatural dreams. Angels also delivered personal messages to select people, who as prophets were to pass on the messages to other people.

6. God revealed Himself through theophanies.

A *theophany* was a visible (and sometimes audible or even tangible) phenomenon by which God personally revealed Himself. Examples include the burning bush, the pillar of fire and cloud, the fire and smoke and lightning of Mount Sinai, etc. These were more direct than the other means of revelation but still were not final. Even more direct were the christophanies, or supernatural appearances of Christ in a sort of preincarnate human form, as in the Angel of the Lord, the Captain of the Hosts of the Lord, the man who wrestled with Jacob, and the Son of God in the fiery furnace. There was also some sort of theophany in Eden (Gen. 3:8). Another form of theophany was the *bath kol*, the voice of God from Heaven, such as the still small voice (1 Kings 19:12), the voice at Christ's baptism and transfiguration, or in John 12:28.

7. God revealed Himself verbally in the Bible.

The next highest form of revelation occurred when God not only spoke through these other means but commissioned certain prophets and apostles to write specific words down. This is the Bible, the verbal revelation of God. Since man's main means of communication is words (greater than gestures, facial expressions, pictures, music, etc.), God used this means to communicate with us. He gave us actual words. These are the very words of God Himself (1 Cor. 2:13). Hence, the Bible frequently describes itself as the Word of God, the words of God, and similar terms.

8. The Bible has several names for itself.

The Bible is called the following: the Book of the Law, the Law, the Law of God, the Ordinances of God, the Law and the Prophets, the Oracles of God, the Testimony, the Word of Truth, and many other such terms. Some terms point out that this verbal revelation was written, not just spoken: the Scriptures, the Holy Scriptures, the Scriptures of Truth, etc. We call it the Bible, from the Latin word *biblia*, which means "book." The fact that God reveals Himself verbally teaches us that God is personal and not an abstract principle. He speaks, therefore is wise. He speaks to us, therefore He cares. Human language is adequate for this level of revelation. God condescended to speak human language.

9. We study the Bible to know God.

It is through the Bible, not nature, that we learn about salvation (Rom. 1:16–17; 1 Peter 1:25). This is how we know God personally. Special revelation is superior to natural revelation and is the means by which we correctly interpret natural revelation. God no longer reveals Himself through dreams, visions, angels, prophets, theophanies, or the direct voice from Heaven. Our job is to diligently study this lasting revelation. To know God better, we must read, study, believe, and obey the Bible. Special revelation has ceased, but the ongoing work of the Holy Spirit, who inspired the Bible, continues. We call this *illumination*, not revelation. The light is on, but we need to have our eyes opened.

10. Jesus Christ is the greatest revelation of God.

Hebrews 1:1–2 tells us that progressive revelation led up to the greatest revelation of God: Jesus Christ. Jesus Himself often said that to see Him was to see God. To know Jesus is to know God. He is the greatest of all revelations, because Jesus is God Himself. He is God in the flesh (John 1:14). He is called "the Word" because He is the greatest revelation of God (John 1:1). He is the personal, living Word of God. This does not demean the value of the Bible but fulfills it. Jesus is now in Heaven. We can pray to Him and love Him, even though we do not see or hear Him directly (1 Peter 1:8). We hear Him when we read His Bible.

7

Inspiration

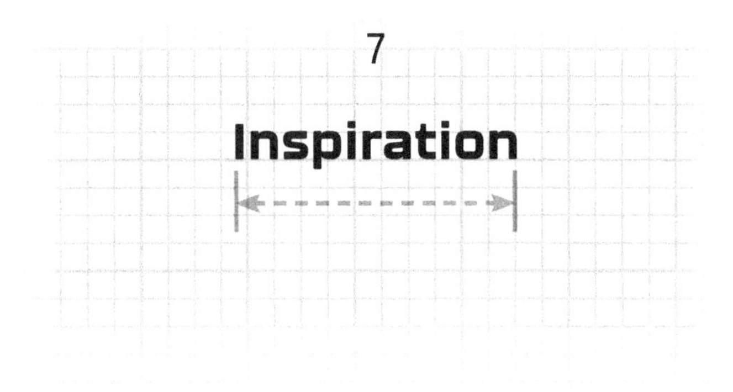

1. The Bible is the Word of God.

The main title that the Bible has for itself is the "Word of God" (John 10:35). This means several things. For one, it is, was, and ever will be God's Word. Its essence and identity have not changed. Also, though God used many people to do the actual writing, it is primarily God's Word. It is not a collection of merely human books (1 Thess. 2:13). It is the Word of God, in contradistinction to certain liberal theories that say it merely becomes, contains, or bears witness to the Word of God. It is the Word of God already, whether we believe it or not. It is already perfect.

2. The Bible alone is the Word of God.

In biblical days, God spoke through prophets, dreams, visions, and angels. But that has ceased. See Hebrews 1:1–2. The Bible continues as the only Word of God. Similarly, preaching is not the Word of God. Preaching should be based on the Bible but is not the same as the Bible. Also, the Bible is qualitatively different from every other book ever written. It alone is the Word of God. It is not one of many divine books, as part of a supposed "Bible of the World" containing the Qur'an of Islam, the Pali Texts of Buddhism, the Rig Veda of Hinduism, the Book of Mormon, and so on. Even the books of the Apocrypha contain only human wisdom. These are not God's Word.

3. The Bible is the written word of God.

God was pleased to commit His word to writing. Hence, it is called "the Holy Scriptures" (2 Tim. 3:15). It was *inscripturated*, or written down in human script. The finger of God directly wrote the Ten Commandments (Ex. 31:18). God used the human authors of Scripture as His fingers to write the Bible (Ps. 45:1). He did this so we would have His word in black and white, in a permanent form to read, study, and consult. We need not depend on a series of priests who passed it on down the ages by word of mouth, to be contaminated by fallible human memory. We have it in writing. Thus, when Jesus appealed to the Bible, He said, "It is written" (Matt. 4:4, 7, 10). It stands written.

4. The Bible is inspired by God.

Second Timothy 3:16 says that all Scripture is "given by the inspiration of God." This is one word in the Greek, *theopneustos*. It literally means "God-breathed." God did not breathe something into the Bible; God breathed the Bible out of His own mouth. Jesus referred to this in Matthew 4:4: "Man shall not live by bread alone, but by every word that proceeds from the mouth of God." When we speak, we exercise our lungs so that they expel air, vibrate our vocal cords, and move our tongue, cheeks, and lips to form sounds we call words. God sent forth the Holy Spirit, the very breath of God (John 3). He moved certain prophets and apostles so that they then put down in writing the exact words God wanted them to write (2 Peter 1:21). Technically speaking, it is the Bible, not the writers, which is inspired. Also, it is inspired because of its source, not its effect. It is not inspired because we feel inspired when we read it. It is divinely inspired regardless of whatever effect it has on us.

5. All the Bible is inspired by God.

Scripture tells us in 2 Timothy 3:16 that *all* the Bible is inspired. Some liberal translations erroneously render this as "every Scripture is also inspired by God," which could imply that the Bible is but one of many inspired books. Rather, the text says that all the Scripture is inspired. This means that all parts are equally inspired. Ruth is as inspired as Romans, Joel as much as John. Therefore, it all carries divine authority and we should read all of it. All parts of it are profitable to our spiritual well-being.

6. The very words of the Bible are inspired.

God breathed out specific words, not just vague ideas or feelings which the human authors were left to interpret and write down. The Bible is verbally inspired. Jesus said, "Every word that proceeds from the mouth of God" (Matt. 4:4). And, 1 Corinthians 2:13 says, "These things we also speak, not in words which man's wisdom teaches but which the Holy Spirit teaches." Indeed, even the very letters of those words were inspired by God (Matt. 5:18). In Galatians 3:16, Paul appeals to the difference of only one letter in the original Hebrew of Genesis 22:18. God inspired the words of Hebrew, Aramaic, and Greek. This does not refer to any translation into English or any other language. Still, the authority of the original language carries over to accurate translations.

7. God controlled the writers of the Bible.

In 2 Peter 1:21 it says that God "moved" certain prophets. The word means "to carry along, to overwhelm by force." They did not simply sit down and decide to write the Bible. God chose who would do the writing, then He worked miraculously in them so that He controlled what they wrote. It was not left to the fallibility of humans. Some parts of the Bible were directly dictated by an audible voice (e.g., Rev. 2 and 3). In most cases, God moved in a deep and mysterious way on their hearts and minds by other methods, such as dreams and visions. They certainly knew that the words they wrote were not merely their own (1 Cor. 14:37). These writers were the keys on God's keyboard, as it were. They were the pens in God's hand (Ps. 45:1).

8. Inspiration is not illumination.

God gave the writers the very words, not just an inner illumination of wisdom. This special inspiration has ceased. What we need now is illumination to understand what has been inspired. The light is on; we need to have our eyes opened. Because of sin, the natural man is incapable of understanding the true meaning of the Bible (1 Cor. 2:14). Jesus said, "He who is of God hears God's words; therefore you do not hear, because you are not of God" (John 8:47). The Holy Spirit who inspired the Bible chooses to illumine whom He will to understand the Bible. And He does this through the Bible itself, for "The entrance of Your words gives light" (Ps. 119:130).

9. God proves that the Bible is the word of God.

Scripture carries with it certain marks of divine authorship. Among them are its high spirituality and morality, its enormous popularity in history, its durability against persecution, and its record of fulfilled prophecy. But these by themselves are insufficient to prove divine inspiration. The Holy Spirit Himself, who inspired Scripture, continues to speak through it (for example, note the present tense “says” in Heb. 3:7). The Spirit is the witness because the Spirit is the truth (1 John 5:6). Even unbelievers are impacted by this power (see Ezek. 2:5). Like the men with Paul on the Damascus road, they hear the sound but do not understand the voice (Acts 9:7).

10. The Bible is powerful.

The Word of God carries with it the very power of God. It is “living and powerful, and sharper than any two-edged sword (Heb. 4:12). It is compared to a hammer that breaks rocks, light that overcomes darkness, fire that cannot be extinguished. It is “the power of God to salvation” (Rom. 1:16). Just as God created all things by the power of His word, so He changes lives today by that same power. God spoke to the prophets and through the prophets. He still speaks today through His Word. Let us listen and be transformed by this powerful book, the Holy Bible.

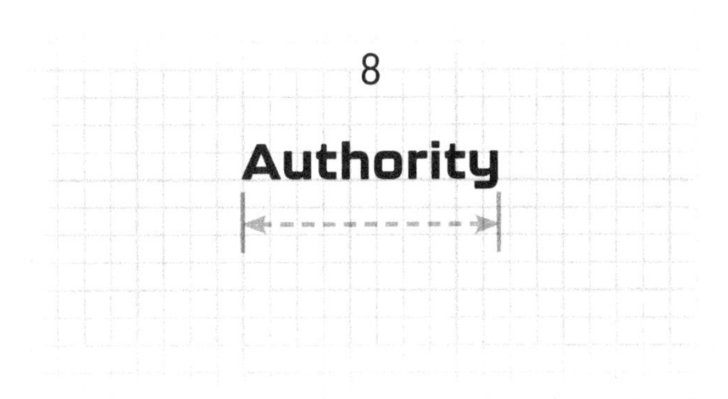

1. The Bible is absolutely true.

The Bible is true. It is also truth itself, for Jesus said, "Your word is truth" (John 17:17). Some other books may be true in that their contents are correct; but only the Bible is truth itself. It is "the word of truth" (Eph. 1:13). It is the only reliable guide to ultimate truth. Many editions of the Bible title it *Holy Bible*, which is quite right, for 2 Timothy 3:15 refers to it as "the Holy Scriptures." Being holy, it is free of all impurity of error. It is pure (Ps. 12:6; 19:8). Indeed, "Your word is very pure" (Ps. 119:140). "Every word of God is pure" (Prov. 30:5).

2. The Bible is inerrant.

The Bible is *inerrant*; it contains no errors. Truth and error are incompatible, like light and darkness. It is also *infallible*; it cannot fail to speak the truth. It does not and cannot err. Jesus said it "cannot be broken" (John 10:35), for all of its individual words are true. Thus, Scripture has no contradictions between its parts, such as the four Gospels. They are complementary, not contradictory. The Bible also contains no myths. Scripture itself warns against myths (1 Tim. 1:4; 4:7; Titus 1:14;

2 Peter 1:16). Parables are not myths. It contains deep mysteries and paradoxes but no errors. Nor does the Bible contain any forgeries or frauds (see 2 Thess. 2:2).

3. The Bible is inerrant in all areas.

The Bible is completely true, in whole and in part, in all details as well as in the general content. It is true whenever it speaks of things we could otherwise study or observe, such as history and science. It is true in all areas, not just the spiritual, religious, and theological. If we do not believe God in the areas we can verify, how could we believe Him in the areas that we cannot verify? (John 3:12). Man can err; God cannot (Rom. 3:4; Titus 1:2). But it is not true that to be human one must necessarily err. Adam did not err before the fall, nor did Christ ever err, and they were fully human. The divine side of Scripture guarantees purity from error in the human side, just as the divine nature of Christ protected the purity of His human side. Yes, the Bible uses round numbers, hyperbole, figures of speech, symbols, and phenomenological language. But these are usual for human language and are not errors.

4. The Bible is true because God cannot lie.

God is truth and cannot lie (Titus 1:2). The Bible is God's word. What Scripture says, God says. Each sentence of the Bible could be prefaced with the phrase, "Thus saith the Lord." The Bible receives its essence and nature from God Himself. This is not to deify the Bible, as we are sometimes falsely accused of teaching. Rather, it is to recognize what God says about His word. To believe the Bible is to believe God. To believe God is to agree that God speaks truth (John 3:33). To charge the Bible with even one error is to disbelieve God and call Him a liar (1 John 5:10). But let God be true and every man a liar (Rom. 3:4). It is dangerous and blasphemous to question the truth of God's word. To judge it is to condemn oneself.

5. The Bible is our final authority.

God tells us to test all things (1 Thess. 5:21). By what? By the Word of God, as the noble Bereans did in Acts 17:11. Anything that contradicts the Bible is automatically wrong (Isa. 8:20). We err if we do not know the Bible or if we contradict it (Matt. 22:29). God tells us "not to think beyond what is written" (1 Cor. 4:6). God curses those who preach false gospels contrary to the one true gospel (Gal. 1:8). *Sola Scriptura*—Scripture alone is our final authority in all areas, such as faith and practice. It carries with it the very authority of God Almighty Himself.

6. The Bible is over church tradition.

In Matthew 15, the Lord Jesus confronted the Jewish religious leaders over the question of authority. They appealed to their tradition; Jesus rebuked them by appealing to Scripture. Church tradition must be subject to the Bible, otherwise it nullifies Scripture. Roman Catholicism repeats the same error as the Pharisees with their tradition. It says that the church gave us the Bible, therefore the church is in authority. But this is wrong. The church is built on God's words, not vice versa (Matt. 7:24). All churches, including all creeds, confessions of faith, catechisms, and church constitutions, are subject to the authority of God's Word.

7. The Bible is over all people.

Men can and do err, but God cannot err. The Bible is therefore over the authority—even the delegated authority—of people who exercise some degree of influence and authority. While Scripture tells us to obey parents, preachers, and politicians, we must obey God and not them if they ever go against the Bible (Acts 5:29). The words and books of theologians, as well as all sermons and Sunday school lessons, must be weighed by the Scripture (Acts 17:11). Any preacher, priest, pope, or rabbi who sets himself up as an equal authority to God is automatically a false prophet, for the true prophets themselves were subject to the authority of the Word of God. There are no exceptions.

8. The Bible is over human thought.

In 2 Corinthians 10:5 we are told to submit all to God and take every human thought captive to the obedience of Christ. Thus, all philosophy, psychology, logic, reason, science, and opinion are subject to the truth and authority of the Bible. Because of common grace, man may learn and teach some truths. But if they contradict Scripture—whether implicitly or explicitly, whether in doctrine or in method—then they thereby condemn themselves as false. This applies to our own thoughts as well. Even Adam before the fall was subject to the spoken word of God. He fell into sin when he rebelled against that authority. The mind of fallen man is still under the authority of God's Word. We dare not trust our fallen minds, which are prone to err.

9. The Bible is over all spirituality.

The Bible is inspired by the Holy Spirit. He never contradicts Himself, for that would be contrary to His nature as the Spirit of Truth. All spiritual feelings, impressions, and intuitions must be subject to the Word. We dare not invent exceptions because we feel that the Spirit is leading us, otherwise we are no different from the fanatic who murders his neighbor with an ax because he felt that God told him to. Nor can any pretended "new revelations" of the Spirit contradict or equal Scripture. Scripture is in authority over our whole being, including experience. Peter himself had heard the *bath kol* voice from Heaven, but stated that we have a "more sure word of prophecy" in the written Word of God (see 2 Peter 1:16–21 KJV). We must "test the spirits," because there are many false prophets in the world (1 John 4:1). The Holy Spirit never contradicts what He says in the Bible. For example, He never "calls Jesus accursed" (1 Cor. 12:3). "If anyone thinks himself to be a prophet or spiritual, let him acknowledge that the things which I write to you are the commandments of the Lord" (1 Cor. 14:37). The Bible alone is our source of all spiritual authority.

10. We must follow Scripture in all things.

We must trust in God and His Word, even when we do not understand it. We must not lean on our own understanding or inclinations (Prov. 3:5). We ought to read it, study it, believe it and obey it. Our attitude to the Bible is to be the same as our attitude to God, for it is His word. This means we are to love it, even as we love God. Love God, love His Word.

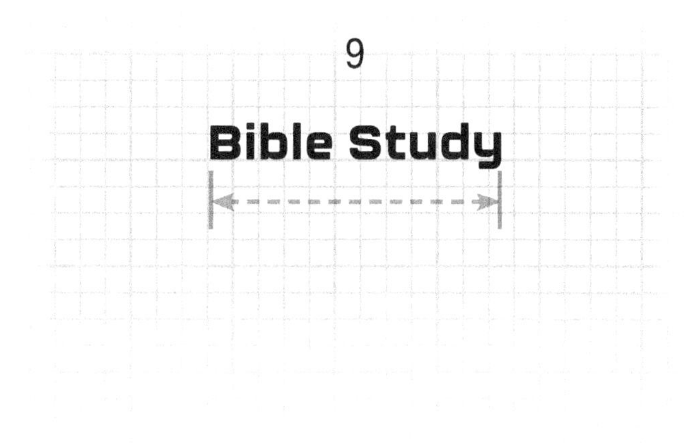

9 Bible Study

1. We should study the Bible.

God gave us the Bible to read and study. It is a textbook to study, not a picture book to browse through. There is a big difference between simply reading a book and seriously studying it. One is leisure, the other is work. God wants us to study our Bibles, not use them for pressing flowers. To study the Bible is to research it to discover its meaning. The term *hermeneutics* is the technical term for the science of interpretation. *Exegesis* is the practice of correct interpretation, by which we draw out of a passage what is really there. The opposite is *eisegesis* or putting into a passage what is not there. That is putting our words into God's mouth, rather than vice versa. Eisegesis is twisting the Scriptures to suit our preconceived notions (2 Peter 3:16).

2. It takes faith to study the Bible.

When we study the Bible, we should set aside wrong presuppositions and preconceived ideas. We need to be teachable. We should pray before and during Bible study, and rely on the Holy Spirit in us to teach us what He says in the Bible. Faith comes to us by the Word of God (Rom. 10:17); more faith comes to us by more Bible study. Without faith, we can understand the Bible only in a natural way, not a supernatural way. Studying the Bible profits us nothing unless it is mixed with faith (Heb. 4:2).

3. It takes work to study the Bible.

We should be like the noble Bereans who "received the word with all readiness, and searched the Scriptures daily to find out whether these things were so" (Acts 17:11). Serious Bible study means to "search the Scriptures" (John 5:39; see 7:52). Search and you will find. Dig deep and you will find new treasures of gold hidden in this field. Like the Bereans, we ought to study the Bible daily as well as diligently. Alas, some Christians have not even read the entire Bible yet. Others try to read it through every year. It takes work, but the Holy Spirit enables us to understand (see 1 John 2:20). We should prepare our hearts "to seek the Law of the Lord" (Ezra 7:10). A lazy attitude betrays low respect for the Bible and little faith in God. But serious Bible study is work which brings rest.

4. The Bible is understandable.

Though the Bible was originally written in Hebrew, Aramaic, and Greek, it is still understandable through reliable translations. We may profit from preachers and teachers who explain the Bible to us (Acts 8:30–31), but we are not held hostage to a priestly caste of guardians who alone can study the Bible. The Bible is for everyone. Though some parts are harder to understand than others (2 Peter 3:16), the basic message of the Bible is quite clear. Even a cursory study of the Bible will yield great results. No one can use the excuse, "I just can't understand it." The Bible uses basic human language. Even its occasional parables, types, and figures of speech are not some kind of hidden code or esoteric allegory. We use the *historical-grammatical method* of Bible study. We study the historical setting of Scripture (human author, original readers, date, geography, manners and customs, archeology, etc.) as well as the normal meaning of the language (its lexical meaning, grammar, syntax, context, etc.).

5. We should study the whole Bible.

We should study all of it, not just our favorite parts. Read both testaments. Use a concordance and cross references to compare Scripture with Scripture. It has great variety. All Scripture is inspired and deserves our study.

6. The Bible uses many literary styles.

Just as God used many human authors, so He used their backgrounds and a variety of literary styles. Much of the Bible is narrative of historical events (Genesis, Joshua to Esther, the Gospels, Acts, much of Exodus and Numbers, parts of others). Other parts are poetry, not prose (Psalms, Job, Proverbs, Ecclesiastes, Song of Solomon, parts of others). In these, we find prayer and praise to God and wisdom in dealing with life. Then other books are mainly laws (Exodus to Deuteronomy, parts of others). Some laws are commands or prohibitions, while others are case laws. Then other books are mainly prophecy, recording direct messages from God, including accurate predictions of the future. There are three *Major Prophets* (larger books like Isaiah, Jeremiah, and Ezekiel) and twelve *Minor Prophets* (the last twelve books of the Old Testament). Some of these books are mainly symbolic and apocalyptic (Revelation, much of Daniel, Zechariah, and Ezekiel, parts of others). Lastly, there are the epistles, or letters, of Paul and others. All these styles form a wonderful harmony.

7. The Bible centers on Christ.

One important principle of Bible study is knowing that Christ is the center of Scripture. The Old Testament pointed forward to Him, the New Testament pointed back to Him. The Old Testament is filled with prophecies, types, and symbols of the coming Messiah (Gen. 3:15; Isa. 53; Ps. 22, etc.). Jesus fulfilled these prophecies. Some are explained in the New Testament (see Luke 24:25–27, 44–46; Acts 10:43). And sandwiched between the Old Testament predictions of the future and the New Testament explanations of the past, we find the four Gospels which describe the person and work of Christ in a special way. They are holy biographies which concentrate on His special person, message, and mission.

8. The Bible teaches us salvation.

Since it is a book about Christ, the Bible is therefore a book about how we may be saved from our sins through Him. It makes us wise unto salvation (2 Tim. 3:15). This message of salvation is given through special revelation in Scripture, not through natural revelation in creation (Rom. 1). Some parts of the Bible more directly discuss salvation, such as the four Gospels, Acts, and Romans. But all parts of Scripture fit into this comprehensive entity. Thus, the Bible was given to us that we may know how to be saved and how to have the assurance of salvation (John 20:31; 1 John 5:13). We can also use it to tell other people the gospel of salvation (1 Peter 1:25).

9. The Bible is spiritual food.

The Bible is frequently compared to food. "Man shall not live by bread alone, but by every word that proceeds from the mouth of God" (Matt. 4:4). We ought to thirst for it like a baby thirsts for milk (1 Peter 2:2). The basic message of the Bible is like milk; the additional details are like meat (Heb. 5:12–14). We need both. The Bible is the means that God uses to nourish His children. It gave us the new birth and sustains our new life. We grow spiritually anemic when we ignore it. So, we need to regularly read and study it, and meditate on it like a cow chews the cud. The more we do this, the stronger we will grow spiritually.

10. The Bible has many uses.

We study the Bible to learn about God. When we study it, we always need to find what God wants us to do in light of that passage. It teaches us how to live for God, helps us resist Satan and temptation, worship God in the way that is acceptable to Him, and witness in the world. It encourages us through its many promises, aids us in prayer, points out our sins and assures us of forgiveness, strengthens our faith, answers the basic questions we have for guidance, and so much more. So let us diligently read it, study it, believe it, and obey it (See Matt. 7:24–25; 2 Tim. 3:16–17; James 1:22).

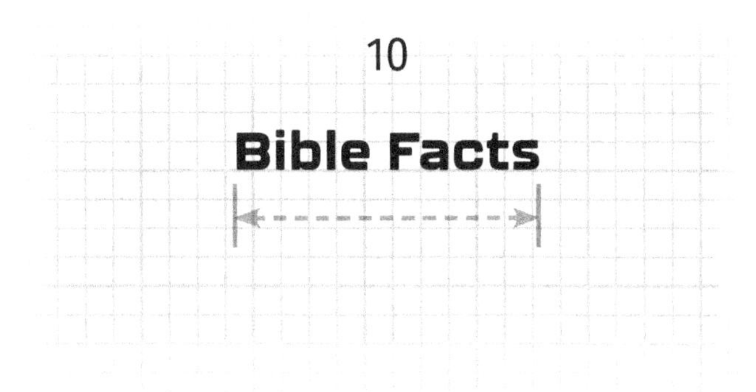

10

Bible Facts

1. The Bible is a unity.

Though it has many individual books in it, the Bible is a unity. It is both one book and many books. It has unity and diversity. It is basically one book, *The Book*. Though it has many human authors for its parts, it is primarily one book by God Himself. God used the many authors over a period of approximately fifteen hundred years to write the Bible progressively, each building on what has already been given. Since it is an infallible unity, all parts agree. The individual authors and books ought not to be seen as contradictory, but complementary to each other.

2. The Bible has two testaments.

The most obvious and significant division in the Bible is that it has two large sections known as *Testaments*. A testament is a covenant, or holy contract, between God and man. The first is the *old covenant*. It makes up about three-fourths of the Bible, of which about a third is by Moses. It revolves around the special covenant which God made with Israel, described in the first five books. The rest of the Old Testament shows how Israel broke that covenant and how God was preparing for a new and better covenant. The Old Testament consists of the Law, the Prophets, and the Writings, or Psalms (Luke 24:44). The New Testament revolves around the *new covenant* which Jesus instituted to replace the old covenant. The New Testament consists of the four Gospels, Acts, the Epistles, and Revelation. The old covenant looked forward to Christ and the new covenant; the New Testament presents Him and the new covenant.

3. The Bible has sixty-six books.

The Old Testament contains thirty-nine books, the New Testament twenty-seven. Psalms is the longest, then Isaiah. Some books are in pairs (1 and 2 Samuel, Kings, Chronicles, and several of the epistles), of which only one is a set of three (1, 2, and 3 John). Luke and Acts form a unique pair. There is occasional overlap of content and matter (e.g., Samuel/Kings/Chronicles, the four Gospels). The books of the Apocrypha are not part of the Bible. Though Roman Catholicism accepts them, neither the ancient Jews nor Protestants have ever accepted them. Nor are any of the books of the Pseudepigrapha in the Bible, such as the book of Enoch, and of course, not the Book of Mormon or other pretended books. The Canon is closed. There are no "lost books" to be found which belong in the Bible.

4. God used many human authors to write the Bible.

Moses wrote more than any other individual, followed by David, Luke (Luke–Acts), Paul, John, and Solomon. Other authors wrote only a single short book. Some of the most famous people in Scripture did not write a book in the Bible, such as John the Baptist, the apostle James, Elijah, Mary, or the Lord Jesus. Some books are anonymous (such as Hebrews). All books were written by men, though two books are primarily about women (Ruth and Esther). The human authors were prophets, priests, kings, apostles, shepherds, generals, a doctor, court officials, and other occupations.

5. The Bible was written in Hebrew, Aramaic, and Greek.

Most of the Old Testament was written in Hebrew, the language of God's old covenant people, Israel. Hebrew is a Semitic language written from right to left, each word based around three consonants, with a grammar and vocabulary very different than English, but much in common with other ancient languages. Parts of Daniel and Ezra, and a few words and verses elsewhere, were written in Aramaic. Aramaic was the *lingua franca* of the ancient Near East until superseded by Arabic. It was very similar to Hebrew. The New Testament was written in *koine* (common) Greek, loftier in ideals than Hebrew. There are also a few Latin and other foreign words.

6. God has preserved the original Bible text.

The actual original parchments and papyri have long ago perished, but the inspired word has been preserved by God through the ages. Jesus promised that His word would never pass away (Matt. 24:35; see 5:18; 1 Peter 1:23–25). We call this *providential preservation*. There are no lost books, sentences, words, or even letters, nor will any yet be found, otherwise they would have been lost until now. Scripture is the means of salvation and the main means of revelation in this age. Its very nature requires its preservation. Satan has tried to destroy it, but the Bible is an anvil that has worn out many hammers. There are over five thousand Greek manuscripts and over one thousand Hebrew manuscripts of the Bible, plus ancient translations and quotations.

7. We should not add to or subtract from the Bible.

Since the Bible is a complete unity, it is very dangerous to tamper with it. God warns against this in Revelation

22:18–19, Deuteronomy 4:2 and 12:32, and Proverbs 30:6. Some English translations are based on the minority of ancient manuscripts which are faulty. They tend to subtract portions such as Mark 16:9–20. A few ancient manuscripts tend to add to the real text, such as the *Codex Bezae*. But the vast majority of manuscripts agree almost in complete detail, so it is wisest to stick to the middle and neither add to on the right side or subtract from on the left side. Nor may we substitute other words.

8. The Bible was first translated into ancient languages.

The first translation probably was done when Jews in Egypt translated the Old Testament into Greek around 200 BC. This is known as the *Septuagint*. Other Greek translations followed. The Jews also produced paraphrased translations of most of the Old Testament into Aramaic, known as the *Targums*. Most were done after the time of Jesus. The Samaritans translated the Pentateuch into their language with alterations. In the early church, there were early translations into Latin, Syriac, Coptic, Gothic, Armenian, Georgian, Ethiopic, and Arabic. Some were better than others and all are useful for study by scholars.

9. There have been many English translations of the Bible.

There have been more translations of the Bible into English than into any other language. First there were bits and pieces by Bede and medieval monks. Then John Wycliffe translated the Bible from the Latin in the fourteenth century. William Tyndale translated the New Testament from Greek and was working on the Old Testament when he was martyred. The sixteenth century saw many other fine translations, especially the Geneva Bible. The Authorized Version of 1611, known as the

King James Version, has been the most popular one in history. Major revisions included the Revised Version, the American Standard Version, the Revised Standard Version, the New American Standard Bible, and the New Revised Standard Version. The New King James Version is a slight revision and is very good. Many others have been weak paraphrases, such as *The Living Bible*, *The Good News Bible*, and *The New English Bible*. The New International Version and the English Standard Version are best-selling evangelical translations. There have also been Jewish and Catholic translations. Overall, over one hundred translations have appeared in English.

10. The Bible is God's Word about Himself.

The Bible is the Book of God. It was inspired by God, written by God through the instrumentality of various human authors, and is primarily about God. It is God's verbal revelation of Himself to us. It talks about man, salvation, animals, the cosmos, and other topics, but mainly about God. Its ethics come from God. Its stories tell how God has worked in history. Its songs sing to and about God. Specifically, it is a book about Jesus, the only mediator between God and man. Praise God for His Word, the Bible.

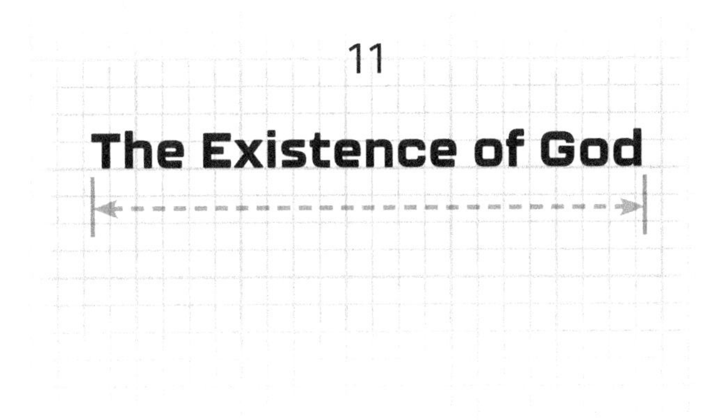

11 The Existence of God

1. God is.

God is. He is there. He is the real God, the God who really exists. He says of Himself, "I AM WHO I AM" (Ex. 3:14). He is the great "I AM." God is God. He exists eternally without origin or change. He self-exists. He has necessary existence, not conditional existence. He really exists, in fact and not merely as a human thought or word. He has perpetual existence in and of Himself. He has pure existence, compared to whom everything else is but a shadow.

2. God is life.

God not only exists, He lives. A stone exists, a person lives. God is the living God, as opposed to the false and dead gods of pagan religions (Jer. 10:10–11). He is life itself—self-life. He has life in Himself, not from another (Acts 17:25). He is the source of all life. He has aseity, or life in Himself (John 1:4; 5:26). He has permanent and perpetual life. God is pure life. Therefore, He is immortal (1 Tim. 6:16). One of the greatest blasphemies ever uttered was the heresy that "God is dead." God cannot die. He had no birthday, therefore no father or mother. He has no death-day, therefore no undertaker.

3. God is uncreated.

God is the creator of everything else (Gen. 1:1). Creator of all, created by none. He is the first cause of everything else but caused by nothing. God is certainly not the creation of man. Man did not create God by imagination, nor by projecting himself to the cosmos, as atheists suggest. Nor is it true that "If God did not exist, it would be necessary to create Him." The nonexistence of God is impossible. Nor is God self-created. He simply exists and lives of Himself.

4. God is not the universe.

The Creator is not the creation. Idolatry worships the creation rather than the Creator (Rom. 1:25). He is separate from His creation. The universe is not an extension of God's being, like an arm or a leg. We are not part of God. Nor is pantheism true when it says, "God is all and all is God." Nor is panentheism true when it says that God is in the universe and the universe is in God. God is everywhere but is not everything. He has a separate and divine substance that is fundamentally different from the universe. God is not an ethereal "force" that permeates all things, as in the New Age movement. Monism is also wrong to suggest that all things are one (i.e., God).

5. All people know that God exists.

Romans 1 and Psalm 19 state that God has made His existence known to all of humanity. We automatically know God exists by a "sense of the divine" kind of internal intuition as well as by external evidence. Those who try to deny this are fools (Ps. 14:1). Therefore, there are no real atheists or agnostics. They already know God exists. They are merely lying in order to run from God. We do not have to prove God's existence to anyone, for they already know it. We merely build upon what God has already revealed about Himself in natural revelation by bringing special revelation. See Acts 17. Indeed, a God whose existence needs to be proved would not be the true God. It is an insult to God to attempt to prove His existence, for that doubts the fact that He has already made His existence known. People already know God exists, but they must acknowledge this openly in order to come to know God personally (Heb. 11:6).

6. God is personal.

God is not an impersonal force or thing. Indeed, God is not a "thing" at all; He is God. Liberals and philosophers think it unbecoming for God to be personal, so they denigrate Him to such things as "the Ground of Being" or "Raw Existence." But God is personal—not exactly like we are personal, but more than we are. Specifically, as we shall see later, God is actually tri-personal in the Trinity. God is a *he*, not an *it*. God is also a *he*, not a *she*. He is the Father, not a mother goddess of pagan religions, such as Mother Earth, Gaia, Sophia, Ishtar, Asherah, and so on (see Jer. 44:17–25). He is personal in that He speaks, feels, thinks, remembers, recognizes, and the like.

7. God is incomprehensible but not inscrutable.

God has told us He exists, and He also gives us the privilege of knowing Him personally. God is knowable. Agnostics and deists are wrong to say God cannot be known. Yet, we can never know everything about God. Finite man can never know all about the infinite God, not even in eternal Heaven. It would take a second God to know God fully. His attributes are beyond full knowledge (Eph. 3:19). God is incomprehensible to us (Job 11:7;

36:26; 37:5; Isa. 40:28; 55:8–9; Rom. 11:33–34; Ps. 71:15; 139:6, 17–18; 145:3; 147:5). There will always be something about God that only God knows (Rev. 19:12). Nor will we know God as God knows Himself.

8. Knowing God is the meaning of life.

Man in sin does not know God (2 Thess. 1:8). God remains "the Unknown God" to sinners (Acts 17:23). The basic message of Ecclesiastes is that life has no meaning, only vanity, without knowing God. God created man to know Him, and man has a dreary existence without knowing God. God has allowed Himself to be known personally. This is only possible through Christ (Matt. 11:27). Knowing God is eternal life (John 17:3), in contrast with meaningless existence.

9. God is perfect.

God is perfect (Matt. 6:48). He is complete in every way. He needs nothing (Acts 17:25). He does not need to be fed (Ps. 50:12). He does not need man. He lacks nothing in any way. He has perfect life and existence and does not grow. He is absolute perfection. He is *actus purus*, "pure actuality," nothing potential or tentative or merely possible. Therefore, God is perfectly happy in Himself. God is not lonely. He did not create man because He was lonely. There was perfect happiness, fellowship, and love within the Trinity (John 17:24). Nothing outside of God is ever perfect in the sense that God is perfect. Yet we find a degree of perfection when we are in the right relationship with God as we ought to be, lacking nothing and happy at last.

10. God is essentially different from us.

There are two truths, which must be kept in balance. On the one hand, God created us in His image (Gen. 1:26–27). Therefore, we resemble God in part. God thinks, we think. God feels, we feel. Specifically, we are to imitate certain attributes of God, which we call the *communicable attributes*. We are to be holy, truthful, and loving, for God is holy, truthful, and loving. On the other hand, God's essence is different from ours. We do not, nor ever can have, self-existence, infinity, eternity, immutability, omniscience, omnipotence, or omnipresence. These are *incommunicable attributes*. God is "wholly other" in His existence. God is not of the same quality as man. He is not a "Big Man"; He is not a man at all. We greatly err in supposing that God is altogether such a one as we are (Ps. 50:21). Even our similarities with God point to the essential differences (we know, God knows; but we know by learning, God knows all things already perfectly, and so on). God exists as only God exists, which is to say God alone is God.

12 The Names of God

1. God can be described but not defined.

God cannot be defined. To define is to limit, but God cannot be limited. Specifically, when we speak or think about God, we cannot fully grasp Him. Therefore, we cannot define God. Yet we can still speak and think of God in part. That means we can describe God. To be precise, God describes Himself to us. He reveals part of Himself to us (description), but not all of Himself (definition). He condescends to describe Himself to us in human analogies, such as metaphors like fire, a fortress, a rock, etc. He also uses *anthropomorphism*, or speaking after the manner of man. God does not literally have arms, legs, a head or other body parts. He even compares Himself at times with animals (wings of a hen, an eagle, a lion, etc.). But God is not an animal or a man. God also uses *anthropopathism*, that is, He describes Himself in terms of human emotions such as love, grief, or anger. But the emotions of God are far greater than ours. So, biblical descriptions are valid. Philosophic definitions are always inadequate (e.g., God is such that nothing greater can be conceived).

2. God names Himself.

God told Adam to name all the animals, but He did not allow him to name God. Names carry a kind of identifying definition in them. But man is not to name God, for that would mean that man is to conceive of God, rather than receive God's revelation of Himself. Moses asked God's name, and God replied, "I AM WHO I AM" (Ex. 3:14). Just as God swears by Himself because there is no one higher (Heb. 6:13), so He describes Himself best by analogy with Himself. God is self-defined. He gives several names in Scripture. Some are used many times, others only rarely. Each is a short description of Himself. Often, they are used together. And there is a name of God which only God Himself knows (Rev. 19:12).

3. God is *Elohim*.

The most common name for God is *Elohim*, such as in Genesis 1:1. It is the plural of a variety of short Hebrew words, such as *El* (Ex. 34:14; Deut. 4:24, etc.), *Eloah* (Job 4:17; 11:7; 19:26; 22:12, etc.), *Elah* (the Aramaic for *Eloah*, Dan. 2:28, etc.), and *Elyon* (usually translated "Most High," Num. 24:16; Ps. 9:2, etc.). *Illai* is a related Aramaic name (Dan. 4:24, etc.). All these indicate greatness or supremacy. *Elohim* is plural but often used with a singular verb, indicating the Trinity. God is Elohim, the great God.

4. God is *El Shaddai.*

Sometimes God uses the name *El* with another one, *Shaddai*. Sometimes He is simply Shaddai. See Genesis 17:1; 28:3; 35:11; 43:14; and 48:3. *Shaddai* means powerful, often translated as "the Almighty." Exodus 6:3 says that God used this name of Himself when revealing Himself to the early patriarchs. There is a corresponding term in the New Testament in Revelation 1:8, the Greek word *Pantokrator*, or "One Able to Do Everything." It is usually translated "Almighty." He is El Shaddai, Pantokrator, the all-powerful One, God Almighty.

5. God is *Jehovah*.

This is the most personal name of all, more a personal name than a title. In Hebrew, it is four consonants, *YHWH*. In older translations, it was rendered *Jehovah*. It is probably better spelled as *Yahweh*. It is often translated as "LORD" in all capital letters. "The LORD is His name" (Ex. 15:3. See Isa. 42:8). Sometimes it is shortened to *Yah* (Ex. 15:2), as in "hallelujah" or "praise the Lord." It speaks of God as the "One Who Is." It is His covenant name. The exact pronunciation isn't vital, nor is it used in the New Testament.

6. God is *Adonai*.

The fourth major name in the Old Testament is *Adonai*, as in Exodus 34:9, Job 28:28, Psalm 2:4, etc. Sometimes it is shortened to *Adon* (Ps. 136:3; Isa. 10:33, etc.). It is generally translated as "Lord," with only the first letter capitalized. It means "lord," "master," "ruler," "owner." "Great is our Lord, and mighty in power" (Ps. 147:5).

7. God is *Theos*.

Coming to the New Testament, we find several names as well. The most common is the Greek word *Theos*. We get the word *theology* from it, the science of God. In the Greek translation of the Old Testament, *Theos* was the usual translation for *Elohim*. It corresponds to the Latin word *Deus*. It was used in ancient Greek literature. But it is not the same as *Zeus*, who was a specific Greek god. The true God is Theos, never Zeus. Like *Elohim*, the word was used in a lesser way to speak of angels and civil rulers, much as the English speak of the House of Lords. But only the one true God is properly Theos.

8. God is *Kurios.*

Kurios is the word in the Greek Old Testament that is usually translated "Jehovah." It means "lord," "master," "owner." In Greek, it could mean "sir" or "master" when speaking of a dignitary. This would be like in Spanish, where a man is called *señor* (mister), and God is called *El Señor* (the Lord). There is only one God and only one Lord (1 Cor. 8:6; Eph. 4:5). God is Lord of all. God is Lord of Lords, thus also King of Kings (1 Tim. 6:15; Rev. 19:16). Two other similar words are used in the New Testament. One is *despotes*, or "total ruler" (Luke 2:29; Acts 4:29; 2 Peter 2:1; Rev. 6:10). The other is *Dunastes*, translated as "Potentate" in 1 Timothy 6:15. But the most common term is *Kurios*, or Lord. Unlike *Jehovah*, it is not all in capitals.

9. God is truth.

God, then, reveals Himself in a variety of short names that describe Himself to us. All of these names are true, even as all of God's revelation is true. This is because God is true. He is the true God, in contrast to the many false gods. He is the real God. He is also truth itself. He speaks truth. Indeed, God cannot lie (Titus 1:2). He always keeps His promises. His Word is inerrant and infallible. He does not deceive. He is trustworthy and dependable, solid and sure. He likens Himself to a rock.

10. God is not the false god of pagans.

There is only one God and He is Lord over all. But that does not mean that He is to be identified with the gods of non-Christian religions. Romans 1 tells us that people worship idols of all sorts. Some are physical images of stone or wood. Others are conceptions formed by man's own imagination. All pagan gods are idols (Ps. 96:5). They are all false gods, not the true God. For example, Allah is not Jehovah. The word *Allah* means "great one," and is an Arabic word similar to the Hebrew *Eloah* and the Aramaic *Elah*. But this does not make Allah the same as the true Elohim. Similarly, Zeus is not the true Theos. Even the Canaanites worshiped a false god named El. What then are these false gods? On the one hand, negatively, they are no-gods, non-divinities, nothings (Gal. 4:8). On the other, they do have an identity. They are demons in disguise. See 1 Corinthians 10:20, Leviticus 17:7, Deuteronomy 32:17, and Revelation 9:20. Pagan religions are merely denominations of one worldwide satanic religion. Vishnu is a demon, Krishna is a demon, Baal is a demon, Isis is a demon, and so on. The Jews give lip service to the one true God, but in rejecting Christ they fall short of knowing the one true God. Through Christ alone we know the one true God.

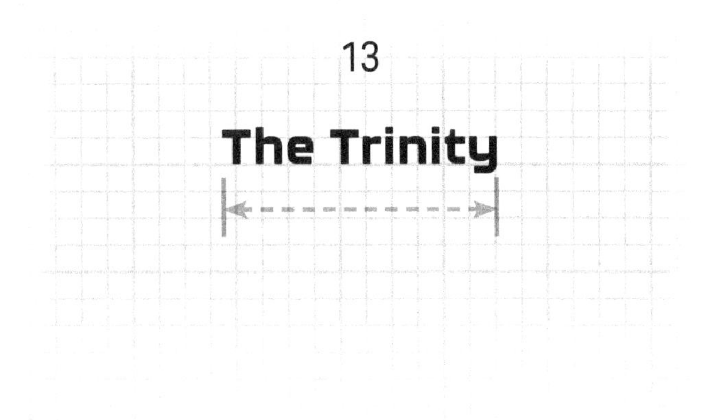

13 The Trinity

1. The Trinity is the mystery of mysteries.

The doctrine of the Trinity is the greatest mystery in the Bible. It is revealed, but not fully revealed. Nor will it ever be fully comprehended by man even in Heaven. It is vastly deep and high and inspires holy awe in those who approach it rightly. It has been accepted by evangelical Protestants, historical Roman Catholics, and the Greek Orthodox. But it has been rejected by many cults, some liberals, and even some Pentecostals, such as the United Pentecostal Church, as well as Jews and Muslims.

2. The Trinity is taught in the Bible.

There is no perfect analogy to the Trinity in creation, so the doctrine is taught by special revelation and not by mere natural revelation. Yet, no one place in Scripture discusses it at length. It is learned by comparing text with text. Still, some places are of particular importance in setting forth the Trinity, such as the baptism of Jesus (Matt. 3) and Christ's command to baptize "in the name of the Father and of the Son and of the Holy Spirit" (Matt. 28:19). All three members of the Trinity are sometimes mentioned together, such as in 1 Corinthians 6:11 and 12:4–6, 2 Corinthians 13:14, Ephesians 2:18 and 3:14–16, 1 Peter 1:2, 2 Thessalonians 2:13–14, and Galatians 4:6.

3. There is only one God.

The first truth of the doctrine of the Trinity is that there is only one God. Perhaps the most important truth of the Old Testament was the *Shema* (Hebrew for "hear") of Deuteronomy 6:4, "Hear, O Israel: The LORD our God, the LORD is one!" This truth is repeated over and over in both testaments. There has always been only one God and always will be only one God (1 Cor. 8:6). The doctrine of the Trinity does not teach that there are three gods. The unity of God disproves *polytheism* (that there are many gods, such as in Hinduism) and *henotheism* (one favorite god among many others).

4. All members of the Trinity are equal.

The Bible also teaches that there is something plural within God. We call them "persons." They share the same one divine nature, the same substance of deity. Thus, all are equal, for one infinite being cannot be larger than another infinite being. There is no hierarchy or subordinate natures within the Trinity. Each one is fully God and has all the attributes of full deity. Each one is God and with God (John 1:1–2). The Son is equal with the Father (John 5:18, Phil. 2:6). Theologians also speak of the Trinity in two ways. The *ontological* Trinity is what God is in and of Himself from all eternity. The *economical* Trinity is the Trinity in relation to time, history, and man. The latter reflects and reveals the first.

5. The members of the Trinity are not identical.

The three divine members share the same nature but have distinct persons. They are not three in the same sense that they are one, so there is no contradiction here. The Father is not the Son, the Son is not the Spirit, and the Spirit is not the Father. There is only one Father, one Son, and one Spirit (Eph. 4:4–6). It was the Son, not the Father nor the Spirit, who became a man (John 1:14). It was the Spirit, not the Son nor the Father, who came at Pentecost (Acts 2:4). The atonement was presented to the Father, not to the Son or to the Spirit. Jesus prayed to the Father in John 17, not to Himself. The Father spoke to Jesus at His baptism; this was no ventriloquism (Matt. 3:17). Jesus called the Spirit "another Helper" in John 14:16, therefore, not Himself. Some groups reject the idea of the Trinity but accept the deity of Christ, saying there is no difference between the three at all. That is known as Oneness Pentecostalism, *modalism*, "Jesus Only," or *patripassianism*. But it is not biblical Trinitarianism.

6. The Father is God.

Matthew 28:19 specifies that the three members of the Trinity are the Father, the Son, and the Holy Spirit. Scripture repeatedly speaks of God as the Father (1 Cor. 8:6). This one is not just Father of Christians, but the Father of the Son (John 17:1). And He is eternally the Father of the Son, not just in the virgin birth. He was Father to the Son from all eternity (John 3:17; 17:5, 24). It was decided in the eternal Trinity that the Father would represent God in His dealings with man, and so the name *God* by itself sometimes refers to the Father. God sent His Son into the world, meaning the Father sent His Son (John 3:17). The Father received the atonement from the Son, who represented man.

7. The Son is God.

The second person of the Trinity is the Son—God the Son. Later we will discuss the deity of Christ more fully. Over one hundred Bible verses prove the deity of Jesus Christ (e.g. John 1:1; 20:28). He is the great "I Am" (John 8:24, 58). He was worshiped as God. Many Old Testament verses that speak of Jehovah are applied to Jesus in the New Testament (Isa. 6:1; John 12:41). Jesus is God, but is not the only person in the Godhead, as taught by the advocates of the "Jesus Only" heresy. There are three divine persons, but only one is the Son.

8. The Son is eternally begotten by the Father.

The distinctive feature of the second person of the Trinity is that He alone is eternally begotten. He is God the Son within the Trinity. This eternal begetting is indicated in John 1:14, 18, 3:16–18, and 1 John 4:9. In theology, it is called *eternal generation*. It is eternal; there was never a time that He was not the Son. Some evangelicals deny this. They say that the term *God the Son* is synonymous with *Son of God*, and that both refer to the incarnation. But Jesus was Son before the incarnation. In fact, the incarnation is the historical display of the eternal nature of the Trinity. Just as a human father has the same nature as his son (e.g., John and Joe Smith are both Smith), so do the eternal Father and eternal Son share the same nature. The Father alone begets the Son. There is no divine mother, no, not even the Spirit.

9. The Holy Spirit is God.

The Holy Spirit is the third person of the Trinity. He is "the eternal Spirit" (Heb. 9:14). There is only one Holy Spirit (Eph. 4:4). He is personal, for He speaks (Heb. 3:7; Acts 13:2); He feels, thinks, and is grieved (Eph. 4:30); He has joy (Rom. 14:17), etc. He convicts of sin (John 16:8–11), regenerates sinners into saints (John 3:5–8), indwells believers, etc. But first of all, the Holy Spirit is God. To lie to the Spirit is to lie to God (Acts 5:3–4), and to blaspheme the Spirit is unforgivable (Matt. 12:31).

The Spirit is God (Isa. 48:16; 63:10; Ps. 51:11; 1 Cor. 3:16; 6:11, 19; 12:4; 2 Cor. 3:17–18, etc.). He is every much eternally God as are the Father and the Son. All three are equal in power, glory, and majesty.

10. The Spirit eternally proceeds from the Father and the Son.

The distinctive feature of the Holy Spirit within the Trinity is what is called *eternal procession*. It is found in John 15:26. It is not the same as the eternal generation of the Son, which comes from the Father, not the Father and the Spirit. The Spirit eternally proceeds from both the Father and the Son (John 15:26). The Greek Orthodox Church says the Spirit proceeds only from the Father. It is difficult to ascertain just what this procession is. It is akin to eternal breathing, thus an eternal *spiration*. This was reflected in the Spirit coming in a special way on the Day of Pentecost like a rushing, mighty wind. He reveals the Father and the Son and stays in the background (John 16:14). Sent by Christ, He is the "Spirit of Christ" (Rom. 8:9; see also Phil. 1:19). He brings the elect to Christ, who brings them to the Father. All in all, the members of the Trinity work together for their mutual glory, which is a display of their perfect unity and diversity.

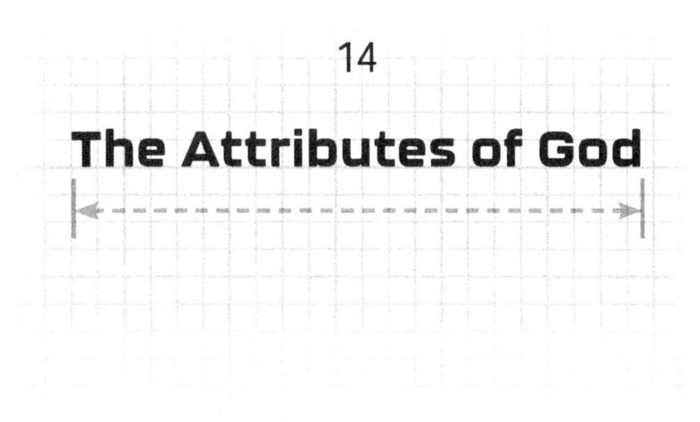

1. God is eternal.

God fills all time and dwells in the realm of eternity (Isa. 57:15). He is the Ancient of Days (Dan. 7:9). He is not only older than the universe, He is eternal. He never had a beginning. He has always been the great "I Am." He is from everlasting to everlasting (Ps. 90:2). He is, was, and always shall be (Rev. 1:8). We cannot fully grasp just what eternity is, though, for we are not eternal. We are limited by time; God is not. God is eternal in His love and other attributes. He gives eternal life, which is not merely endless life but eternal in its quality.

2. God is infinite.

God is not limited by time; neither is He limited by space. He is infinite. He is omnipresent, or present everywhere at the same time. He is immense. God is not only big; He is "sizeless." There is no place where God is not. He is a circle whose center is everywhere and whose circumference is nowhere. The entire universe cannot contain Him (1 Kings 8:27). The universe, therefore, is not infinite, but God is. He is everywhere, but especially in Heaven.

Also, He is imminent, or near all of us (Acts 17:27). He is also transcendent, or high above us (Isa. 57:15).

3. God is spirit.

God is spirit, not a spirit (John 4:24). This refers to His being, not the Holy Spirit. God has no material body. His substance is pure and uncreated spirit. He is invisible to us now, but one day we will see Him (Matt. 5:8). Being pure spirit, He is one in being, not having parts. The attributes of God are not parts of God, but qualities of His whole being. The Mormons are wrong to say God has a physical body. It is true that God the Son became a man and took on a fleshly body (John 1:14), but this is not the same thing.

4. God is unchangeable.

God is perfect and, therefore, never changes (Mal. 3:6; Job 23:13). There is no shadow of change in His being (James 1:17). He is immutable. He cannot change for the better, for He is already perfect. Nor can He change for the worse, for that would mean He is not perfect. He is not growing, either. So-called process theology says God is changing and growing. But God already knows everything and is everywhere, so He cannot change to a fuller existence. This does not mean He is stagnant, though. He is perfect in life. And God does not change His mind or decrees. He is the same yesterday, today, and forever (Heb. 13:8). Everything else changes, but not God (Heb. 1:12).

5. God is holy.

God is holy (Isa. 6:3). He is absolutely pure. "God is light and in Him is no darkness at all" (1 John 1:5). He is absolutely morally pure. It is not that He became pure by purification, but is pure by nature. He is totally just. His will is law for all His creatures, but there is no higher law to which God is subject. Also, because we are not holy, God is angry (Ps. 7:11). He is filled with wrath and fury, far more than we can imagine (Nah. 1:2). And it is a pure and holy wrath, not like losing one's temper. God is so holy that He cannot break His own law. It is the height of blasphemy, then, for any mere sinful creature to accuse God of doing anything wrong. Being angry against sin, God will punish all unrepentant sinners in eternal Hell (Rev. 14:10–11). Lastly, we are to pattern our ideas and lives after God, for He has said, "Be holy, for I am holy" (1 Peter 1:16). We should strive to obey Him in all things without hesitation or question.

6. God is sovereign.

God is the King of Kings (1 Tim. 6:15). He is the absolute ruler of the entire universe (Ps. 103:19). He is the just potentate of everything and is subject to nothing and nobody. He is absolutely free and independent. He does whatever He wants to (Ps. 115:3; 135:5–6; Job 23:13; Dan. 4:25). He owns everything and does whatever He wants to with it. He rules as king over all (Ps. 93:1). He is the supreme Judge, above whom there is no appeal. Therefore, no one can accuse God, for He is the Potter, and we are the clay (Rom. 9:20–21). Is it not His right to do whatever He wants with His universe? (Matt. 20:15).

7. God is powerful.

God is omnipotent, or all-powerful. He is God Almighty (Gen. 17:3). He has all power and strength. He has all life and energy within Himself and supplies life and energy to His universe (Acts 17:25). Being omnipotent, there is nothing too hard for Him to do (Gen. 18:14). It is blasphemy to even suggest stupid questions like, "Can God make a rock too heavy for Him to lift?" He is pure power. He never grows tired nor sleeps (Ps. 121:4). Even when He ceased creating all things, He was not resting from fatigue (John 5:17; Gen. 2:2). Being the highest and perfect God that He is, He has this infinite power from within Himself, not from outside Himself.

8. God is wise.

God is omniscient. He knows all things (Ps. 147:5). He knows every detail of everything that is, was, or ever shall be. He also knows every possibility of things that could be but never will be (Matt. 11:21–23). He knows all answers to all questions. He makes no mistakes. He remembers everything. He never learns, for He has always known everything about everything. He knows the future (John 13:19). It is gross heresy to say that God "limits His knowledge," as if God could choose to not know something He already knows. He says He "forgets" our sins by way of justice, not by way of omniscience. God is also perfectly wise. He knows what is best. He knows all relationships between facts and how they work out together for the planned end. Finally, God has perfect self-knowledge.

9. God is love.

God is love (1 John 4:8). First, God loves Himself. The Father, Son, and Holy Spirit all love each other perfectly (John 17:24). God is not lonely. But God expresses this internal love externally to His creatures (John 17:24). He has a general love for all things as creatures. But He also has a special love for His people, which is called election (Rom. 9:11). Theologians speak of God's "love of benevolence" (love for the unlovely) and His "love of complacence" (love for the lovely). He has grace for the guilty, mercy for the miserable, kindness for the helpless (Eph. 2:4). God is good. He is patient. God is generous (James 1:5). He is compassionate. He is forgiving. These and many other terms are used to say that "God is love."

10. God is glorious.

God is all glorious within. He is the God of glory (Acts 7:2). Within the Trinity, there has always been an infinite splendor of light and glory that we have never seen or known (1 Tim. 6:16). It is the glory of God. It is His plan to reveal this internal glory externally to His creation. This glory will one day be revealed and reflected in all things. His love will be displayed in His elect and His wrath in the non-elect (Rom. 9:22–23). In turn, this revealed glory will be reflected back to God. In that sense, we are said to give glory to God (Ps. 29:1). What is the glory of God? It is His splendor, His fame, His beauty. It is the revelation of what He is, all that He is, all His attributes together in perfect harmony. It is often compared to light in all its various refracted colors, like the rainbow. It is living glory. And the focal point of it is the Lord Jesus Christ, through whom God reveals His glory to creation, and through whom He receives it back again.

15

The Plan of God

1. God has a plan.

The universe is not a car without a driver, nor a driver without a map. There is a purpose behind everything (Eccl. 3:1). The Bible often speaks of this great plan of God. It is the "purpose" of that famous Bible verse, Romans 8:28. God has planned out this purpose in advance. He thought it out, planned it in every detail, and carries it out "on purpose." It is an absolute purpose, not merely a wish or command. In theology, it is called the *decree*. God has decreed His purpose and it shall happen. See Romans 9:11, Isaiah 46:10–11, Ephesians 3:11, Acts 4:28, and 2 Timothy 1:9.

2. God predestined everything.

The plan of God is also called *predestination* or *foreordination*. God preprogrammed everything that will come to pass (Eph. 1:11). Everything can be traced back to God's ultimate plan, "for of Him and through Him and to Him are all things" (Rom. 11:36). He not only created all things (Gen. 1:1) but drew up the blueprints for everything. He foreordained what will happen, and He did this in advance in eternity. He drew up the plan before He laid the foundation. He predetermined what would happen, not merely what could or should happen. Then He set the ball rolling in a certain course and it must follow the prearranged course.

3. God planned every detail.

There is a time for every purpose under Heaven, says Ecclesiastes 3:1. God has planned out this great purpose to the smallest detail. This includes the exact timing when everything would occur. He also prepared every relationship with every other detail. Nothing was ignored. Even the smallest and seemingly insignificant detail was included, such as the number of hairs on our heads. He prepared this detailed inventory in advance and the construction of the universe follows it perfectly, for God is the great architect and contractor who never makes a mistake. In theology, we speak of the great plan as the "decree" and the individual details as "decrees."

4. There is no such thing as chance.

Since God has determined everything in advance, there is no such thing as chance. "Chance" was a concept invented by certain Greek philosophers, especially promoted among the Epicureans (opposed in Acts 17). It denies the existence of a personal and sovereign God who foreordains everything. Similarly, there is no such thing as luck, either good or bad. Nor is there any fortune or accidents. Even the roll of dice has been determined by God (Prov. 16:33). Conversely, there is also no such thing as blind fate, a concept promoted by the ancient Stoics. Whatever will be will be, but only because God has determined it so. Coincidence is true only in the sense that two events may coincide or happen at the same time. But that is because God planned it like that.

5. God's plan is inevitable.

This plan will, shall, and must come to completion. It is inevitable because God is sovereign and omnipotent. Neither angel, demon, sinner, nor saint can stop it in any detail, for even their actions to stop it are part of the plan. Nothing can stop it. See Psalm 33:11, Titus 1:2, Proverbs 19:21, Isaiah 14:27, Hebrews 6:17, and Job 42:2. It is God's plan and only God could change it. But God has sworn with an oath that He will not change it. He is not fickle like a man who can change his mind (1 Sam. 15:29; Jer. 4:28; 23:20; 30:24). In time, God interacts with us and seems to change His mind (Jonah 3:10), but this is all part of the great strategy. The plan is God's eternal purpose and God does not change His sworn intentions (Ps. 110:4). He is not a cheat. He keeps the oath He has sworn.

6. God consulted only with Himself in the plan.

This should be obvious, since nobody else existed when God made the plan. He did not consult with the angels, for they are not on the same level as God. He consulted only with Himself within the Trinity (Eph. 1:11; Ps. 33:11). Who is able to serve as advisor to God on such things (Rom. 11:34; Isa. 40:13–14)? God did not consult with man even by foresight, for He foresaw what He predetermined would occur. When it comes to pass, then, only God can take the credit for the accomplishment of what was planned.

7. God has not revealed all the details of the plan.

"The secret things belong to the LORD our God, but those things which are revealed belong to us and to our children forever, that we may do all the words of this law" (Deut. 29:29). God has revealed that there is a plan and has even revealed a few details of the plan (Eph. 1:9). But He has not revealed it all, nor could we comprehend it all even if He did. We must not pry into things that have not been revealed, such as the date for the second coming of Christ (Mark 13:32). In theology, we speak of the plan as the *secret will* of God. On the other hand, God has revealed much to us about our responsibility. This is the *revealed will* of God. Though God is sovereign and has foreordained all our thoughts and actions, we are still accountable and responsible (Luke 22:22). The revealed will includes the law and the gospel.

8. God uses even sin in His plan.

Even sin is included among the details of the great plan. How could it be otherwise? Sin infects and affects so much of human existence, and much of the plan directly concerns man. Therefore, God included sin in the great plan. He uses sin and sinners to carry out His purpose, even their own destruction (Prov. 16:4). We sinners mean sinful things for evil, but God means them for good (Gen. 50:20). God not only overrules sin, but includes it in a marvelous way as part of the plan. He planned to allow sin in order to reveal His holiness and justice in punishing it or to reveal His grace and mercy in forgiving it (Rom. 9). Even the crucifixion of Christ, the worst of all sins, was predestined by God (Acts 2:23; 4:28).

9. Christ is central to the plan of God.

The plan is *Christocentric*. Christ is the very apex of God's purpose, for it is through Christ that God reveals His glory and through Christ that God receives glory back from His creation. Colossians 1 describes how Christ is preeminent above all things, prominent in the plan of God and the great pivot of all history. Philippians 2 also describes how Christ is the center of God's plan, specifically the plan of redemption. We are not saved merely to enjoy God forever; we are saved in order to give glory to Christ and through Him give glory to the Father.

10. God's plan is to reveal His glory.

Romans 11:36 says that all things are from God in predestination and creation. They are also through Him in providence. But they are also to Him in the final accomplishment of the great plan. And the bottom line of this plan is just this: the glory of God. God does all things for His own glory. Everything that is, was, or ever shall be will give glory to God (Ps. 46:10; 145:10). God will reveal His glory when it is time for the great consummation. He will show His glory—glory revealed. He will receive glory reflected back to Him—glory received. God does not share His glory with another (Isa. 42:8; 48:11). Yet He does show His glory in part now and more fully in eternity. He will display the glory of His grace to the elect (Eph. 1:6, 12, 14) and the glory of His wrath to the reprobate (Rom. 9:22). And this glory will even be revealed to the angels, demons, and inanimate objects. To God be glory forever and ever!

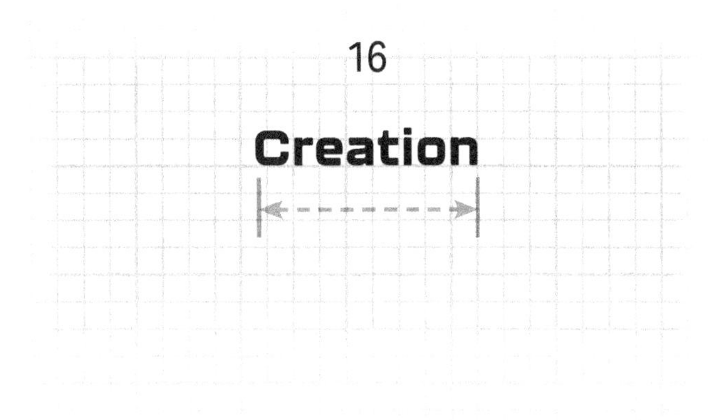

1. God created the universe.

The first verse of the Bible states one of the most important truths in the whole Bible: "In the beginning God created the Heavens and the earth" (Gen. 1:1). God is the Creator. He is our "Maker" (Isa. 54:5). The universe did not create itself; it was created by God (Ps. 100:3). God has revealed this great truth through the things which are created (Rom. 1:18–20). Each member of the Trinity was involved in creation (Gen. 1:1–2; John 1:3).

2. God created the universe out of nothing.

Before creation, God alone existed (Ps. 90:2). When He created the universe, therefore, He could have created it out of Himself (which the Bible denies) or out of sheer nothingness (which the Bible teaches). He merely spoke it into existence (Gen. 1; Heb. 11:3). This is the power of His word and the word of His power (Heb. 1:3). We say He created all things *ex nihilo*, or out of nothing. We cannot comprehend this; there is no adequate analogy in nature. When an artist paints a picture, he does not really create it out of nothing. God created all things, but not all at once. He did it in stages.

3. God created the universe in six days.

Genesis 1 describes the period of creation as six days of "evenings and mornings." In the Hebrew way of speaking, sundown is the start of a new twenty-four-hour day. While some Christians wonder if these were literal twenty-four-hour periods or symbols of periods of much greater length, we point out several things. First, the Hebrew word *yom* almost always means twenty-four-hour days. Also, Genesis 1 uses the normal description of evening and daylight markers. Perhaps most conclusive is that the time periods are equal in length—and man was created on the sixth day. If the first five were millions of years old, then Adam would have to have been ancient indeed! Exodus 20:11 says that the seventh day became the pattern for the weekly sabbath.

4. God created things on different levels.

Genesis 1 describes how God created things from the simpler to the more complex. First, He created the raw stuff of the universe: matter, light, and energy. Then He created inanimate things. Then plants, animals, and finally man. There are variations and subdivisions within these categories, such as gases, subatomic particles, and amoebas. These levels display God's "order" (see 1 Cor. 15:39). We might add that Genesis 1 is describing the creation of the natural side of the universe, not the supernatural. God created the angels first, for they were witnesses of the creation of the physical universe (Job 38:4–7). God alone created the universe. The angels may have been messengers or assistants in the work of the natural part, but they were not creators.

5. There is no movement between created levels.

The things on each level interact with each other, but there is no climbing the ladder of created levels. For example, a cow may eat grass, but grass does not evolve into cows. Man drinks water, but water does not evolve into man. Hence, the idea of evolution is quite wrong. Rocks don't become dogs, horses don't become humans, humans don't become angels. The New Age movement, eastern religion, and some aspects of evolution theorize that all things are evolving upward along this ladder of existence, resulting in Godhood. This is very wrong. We were created by God, but not out of God. We were created for God, but not to become God. Reincarnation says we go up and down this ladder, but that too is quite wrong. Of course, there is variation within each level, and some forms become extinct, such as the dodo bird and dinosaurs.

6. Creationism disproves the theory of evolution.

The theory of evolution is not merely a scientific theory; it has religious overtones and implications for theology. Simply put, it contradicts Genesis 1 and is therefore erroneous. It suggests that before a "Big Bang," there was nothing. Then there was amorphous gas, space foam, cosmic soup, or something like it. Then by mere chance, it developed by itself into the universe and has been growing ever since. That's not what God says. First, there is no such thing as chance. Second, God created things on several levels at the beginning and in a short period of time. Third, the order of Genesis 1 is different from the order suggested by all evolutionists. Evolution is just a theory (and unscientific at that) whose main objective is to eliminate God. So-called theistic evolution is an erroneous attempt to say that God used evolution in creation. But this is also unbiblical on many points.

7. God ceased creation after the first week.

God rested on day seven (Gen. 2:2). This does not mean He was tired, for God has all power and had no less power when He created the universe than before. He never tires (Isa. 40:28). He ceased creating, and so has not created any new levels. He began the work of sustaining His creation, which we call *providence*. Through providence, He keeps His creation in existence, develops it, guides it, and so on. But there are no new acts of creation, except in the spiritual realm. The new birth is called a "new creation" (2 Cor. 5:17). Even so, it is not creation out of nothing per se. It simply means that God does not save us by reforming the old man, but by forming a new man within us by regeneration.

8. Man's sin affected the universe.

God created the universe and pronounced it "very good" (Gen. 1:31). It reflected His glory and was free from sin. The sin of Satan had already occurred in the invisible, nonmaterial, supernatural side, but that did not affect the material universe—until he successfully led Adam and Eve into sin. This brought a curse on creation (Gen. 3:17–18). This is why there are now storms, earthquakes, tornadoes, volcanoes, droughts, famines, wild animals, plagues, and death (Rom. 8:20–22). None of these were part of the original creation. The levels of things below man are incapable of sin, but suffer the consequences of our sin. Incidentally, Gnosticism wrongly said that matter itself is necessarily evil.

9. God sent a worldwide flood to judge sin.

Sin proliferated at a rapid pace after Adam and Eve. Then there was an invasion of demons in Genesis 6:1–4. It got so bad that the cup of wrath was filled, and God judged the whole world. He started all over, as it were, by flooding the earth and making it resemble the way it was in Genesis 1:2. Only eight humans were spared to start the human race again (1 Peter 3:20), but they brought sin with them into the ark. Two of every kind of animal were brought on the ark, so God did not begin creation entirely anew as in Genesis 1. This massive flood covered the whole world and caused enormous changes in the earth's landscape and weather, among other things (2 Peter 3:6). Thus, the flood was unique. Such a flood has never occurred since, nor ever will again (Gen. 9:11). It was the greatest catastrophe since creation.

10. God will one day re-create the universe.

The flood was only a partial re-creation. Sin left the ark and began to multiply again (Gen. 9:21). The material universe was still cursed. God's glory in nature is still marred by sin and its effects. But not for long. Jesus Christ came to save man. Some men will be saved. Through that redemption, the curse on creation is lifted. One day, at the second coming of Jesus, the effects of the curse will be erased in the new Heavens and the new earth (Rev. 21:1; Isa. 65:17; Rom.8:21; Acts 3:21). It will reflect God's glory perfectly, far greater even than in Genesis 1.

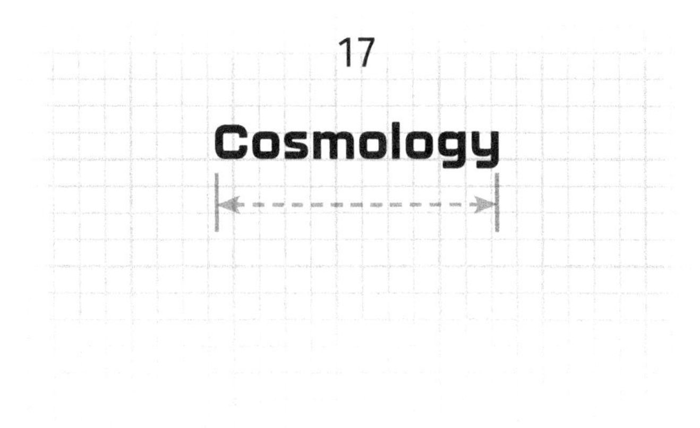

17 Cosmology

1. God created time.

God is eternal and inhabits eternity (Isa. 57:15). We cannot really grasp eternity as such, since we are not eternal. But we can understand it a little by contrasting it with time. It would seem that eternity is an "eternal now," unlimited by the boundaries of time as we know it. It is more than time without beginning or end. God alone is eternal. He created time. This is implied in Genesis 1:1 and John 1:1. In the beginning of creation, God already existed. He was before time and therefore created time at the beginning of the creation of the universe (2 Tim. 1:9). Since, by definition, time is not eternity, time had a beginning, which is creation. Since God is the creator of all things created, God created time.

2. The universe is relatively young.

How old, then, is the universe? How long ago was "the beginning" of Gen. 1:1? As we saw before, the days of Genesis 1 were twenty-four-hour periods, not eons of millions of years, let alone eternity. That is a major marker for our determining from the Bible how old the universe is. God also gave other useful markers in the

Bible, especially the genealogies of Genesis, Chronicles, Matthew, Luke, and a few other places. Many of these specify how old people were when they had certain children and how old they were when they died. Other passages indicate the time periods of the captivities in Egypt and Babylon, the desert wandering, and the period between the Old and New Testaments. Putting them all together, we discover that creation occurred about six thousand years ago. The minor gaps in the genealogies were after Abraham, not before. A general chronology to remember would be this: Adam (4000 BC), Noah (2500 BC), Abraham (2000 BC), David (1000 BC), Jesus (2000 years ago). Also, there is no truth to the so-called gap theory— namely, that there was a gap of millions of years between Genesis 1:1 and 1:2. That is an unnecessary accommodation to evolution and suggests there was death in the world before Adam (contrary to Rom. 5:12).

3. The universe is not God.

The universe is creation, not the Creator. It is not self-created (Ps. 100:3). It does not have a soul. It is not composed of divine substance, for God created it out of nothing and not out of Himself. It is not eternal; it is relatively young. It is not infinite. God alone is infinite and omnipresent. The Heavens and earth cannot contain the infinite God, and so it is not infinite (1 Kings 8:27). Contrary to philosophers such as Plato and Bertrand Russell, the universe is not eternal. On the other hand, the universe is real. It is not a figment of our imagination, as taught by Buddhism and Christian Science. It exists because God created it.

4. The universe has two parts.

Colossians 1:16 says that the universe has two parts or sides: the natural (Heavens and earth) and the supernatural. One is visible, the other invisible. One is subject to scientific observation through our five senses, the other is not. The Bible says that there are three Heavens: the atmosphere around the earth, outer space, and the immediate presence of God. The first two are natural, the third is supernatural (2 Cor. 12:2). Angels live in the supernatural realm.

5. God created the universe with order.

God is a God of order and displays this order in creation. It is not chaos. There is still order in spite of sin. He called the world "good." It is complicated, vast, and wonderfully made (Ps. 139:14). There are levels of order, and the glory of God is revealed in each in a wonderful manner (1 Cor. 15:40).

6. God created natural law.

Part of the order which God has built into His creation is what is known as *natural law*. It includes what we call "the laws of science," but more. The Declaration of Independence refers to "the Laws of Nature and of Nature's God." These scientific principles indicate God's moral order. This is that part of general revelation in which God uses the scientific order to reveal morality. Thus, Romans 1:26 says that homosexuality is not only sinful but "unnatural." It is against nature. Heterosexual fornication is wrong, but not "against nature" as such. In 1 Corinthians 11:14, God says that it is unnatural and therefore wrong for men to have long hair like a woman. "Does not even nature itself teach you . . . ?" This natural law overlaps with the law written on our consciences (Rom. 2:14–15).

7. The universe is a network of spheres.

God created the universe as a network of overlapping and intersecting aspects which we might call *spheres*.

They would include things such as numbers, time, space, mind, life, matter, symbolism (such as language), value (such as money), justice, faith, ethics, and beauty. There are similarities and differences between them all. The more we study them, the more we are amazed at the complexity and wonder of God's creation.

8. God delegated authority to man over the universe.

Genesis 1:26–30 describes the *creation mandate* which God gave to Adam and Eve and their descendants. God made us stewards over His creation. We have dominion over the earth. This was not abolished by the fall, only made more difficult. Nor was it abolished or fulfilled by redemption. We are still to use the world which God created for His glory. Thus, we can kill and eat animals, mine minerals, build buildings, and start schools. This is a *cultural mandate* to develop the culture of creation. We are to work and produce. The world does not exist for itself or for our own luxury. We may not despoil it, but must use it properly.

9. Man is to use the world to God's glory.

The purpose of creation is to display God's glory (Rom. 11:36; Ps. 19:1). Unfallen man was to cultivate the world unaffected by sin for this end. The fall made it more difficult, but not impossible. God grants us common grace to carry out this dominion mandate in part. The end is still the same: the glory of God. All we do is to be productive and to further the glory of God (1 Cor 10:31; Col. 3:17). We are to work at our jobs as if Christ were our employer, for ultimately He is (Eph. 6:5–8). We study at school for His glory, we raise our families for His glory, we are involved in society for His glory. The Bible is our guideline and grace is the enabler.

10. We must worship the Creator, not the creation.

God created the world for His glory, and He does not share His glory with anyone or anything, even His creation (Isa. 42:8; 48:11). He displays glory in and through it, but we are to worship the Creator and not the creation (Rom. 1:25). It is the mark of idolatry to worship nature rather than nature's God. It is also idolatry to worship nature as God, such as Mother Nature, Mother Earth, pantheism, etc. It is easy to admire the beauty of nature, but we must not allow ourselves to forget that God put that beauty there as a reflection of His beauty and glory. We should see that glory and reflect it back to God. To ignore God in it is to fall into idolatry. God warned the Jews not to worship the stars of Heaven (Deut. 4:19). We should use nature to worship nature's God. Thus, worship is not only spiritual (e.g., prayer and Bible reading), but material. We worship God at work when we do good work. To use nature for ourselves is a form of self-idolatry. Let us worship the Creator in all we do with all He has made.

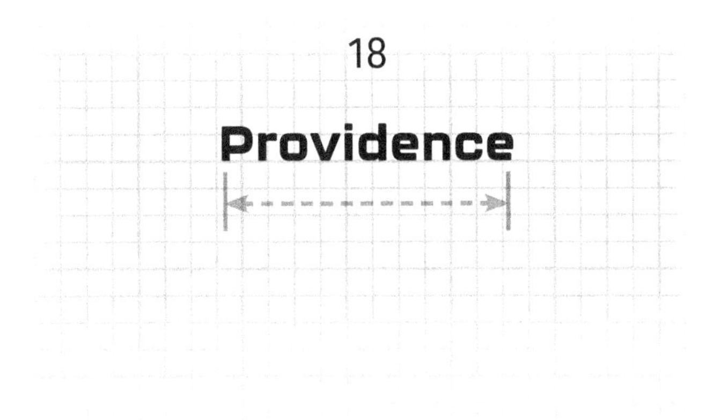

18 Providence

1. God is involved with His creation.

Creation was the beginning, not the end, of God's involvement with the universe. God takes an active interest and involvement with His creation. He is not an absentee landlord, as suggested by eighteenth-century deism. He did not wind it up like a clock and step back and let things take their course. He not only knows what is happening throughout the universe but is involved in every detail and the relationships between everything. Sometimes He uses angels to carry on the work, sometimes He acts normally, sometimes unusually. But He never is absent or ignorant. God is in charge.

2. God upholds all things.

"Through Him . . . are all things" (Rom. 11:36). God predestined and created all things and guides them every moment along their foreordained ways to the culmination of all things. Nothing goes astray from the prearranged plan. He also "uphold[s] all things by the word of His power" (Heb. 1:3). Just as He created everything by His word of power, so He sustains everything by this same word. He does not continue to create things, but keeps them existing so that they do not fall into nonexistence. He sustains all things; in Him all things consist or hold together (Col. 1:17).

3. God provides for the universe.

Everything depends on God for existence and all the relevant details of space and time. He provides all energy for the atoms, lightning, electricity, magnetism, gravity, light, etc. He also is the source of all life. "He gives to all life, breath, and all things . . . for in Him we live and move and have our being" (Acts 17:25, 28). God feeds the animals (Matt. 6:26). He preserves all living things (Ps. 36:6) and provides life to all living creatures (Neh. 9:6). He provides through providence.

4. God allows catastrophes.

God allows what we would call natural disasters and tragedies. For example, God is in complete control of the weather (Job 38:25–38). There is no "Mother Nature." Even insurance companies refer to "acts of God" beyond the foresight or influence of man. God allows floods, droughts, tornadoes, hurricanes, blizzards, earthquakes, and so on. Part of this is because of the curse on creation due to the sin of man. Some disasters are due to specific sins, others not. God allows airplane crashes, burning homes, birth defects, financial ruin, and broken marriages. These are not outside His dominion. He cannot be blamed, however, nor should we ever even think of blaming Him when they strike us. God allows wars, revolutions, and corrupt governments. He allows all these to remind us of sin and warn us of future judgment.

5. God loves His creatures.

God loves His creation, especially the higher they are on the levels of creation. He loves humans more than animals (Matt. 6:26). He has a general love for all people as His creatures made in His image. This is part of common grace. In this sense, God loves everyone (Ps. 33:5). God created us out of love and this continues even after the fall in spite of sin. Thus, it is common grace, not just a general love. God tells us to love our enemies, because God Himself loves His enemies (Matt. 5:44–45). This flows from God's very nature as love itself (1 John 4:8).

6. God sends good to all His creatures.

We must do good to all men, because God does good to all men (Matt. 5:44–45; Luke 6:35–36). He sends rain and sunshine on all people, regardless of whether they are Christians or not (Acts 14:17). Everything good in the world is a gift from God the Creator to His creatures (James 1:17; 1 Tim. 4:4; Gen. 1:31). He even gives good things to people that end up in Hell (Luke 16:25). He rarely is ever thanked for these gifts, for ingratitude characterizes fallen man (Rom. 1:21).

7. God takes special care of His children.

There is a general providence for all men and a special providence for the elect, before and especially after their conversions. God tells us to love and do good for all men, especially other Christians (Gal. 6:10). God does the same here. This is why God works all things together for good for those who love God and are called according to His purpose (Rom. 8:28). It does not always appear such, especially in the midst of trials and afflictions and disasters. But we need to be patient and have faith. One day all will be explained to us. We need not fret because the righteous suffer and the wicked prosper, for this is only temporary (Ps. 37:1–2). God is in complete control and takes a special interest in His children.

8. God is involved in human hearts.

God is totally sovereign in providence, even in the hearts and wills of man. Our will is not off-limits to God. He can intervene and interrupt at any time. Indeed, He regularly does this. He gives faith, and He withholds faith. He overrules the plans and desires of our minds (Prov. 16:1, 9). He turns our hearts like rivers (Prov. 21:1). He puts things like joy in our hearts (Ezra 6:22; 7:27). He works all things in all persons (1 Cor. 12:6). He is at work on our wills so that we will and do what He wants (Phil. 2:13). This is a deep mystery. God is sovereign, but we are still responsible. Theologians call this *concurrence*. God mysteriously guides our very thoughts and motives, good and bad, in such a way that He is sovereign and cannot be blamed, while we are still responsible.

9. God restrains sin.

God is even in control of sin. Sometimes He restrains us from sinning (Gen. 20:6). He prevents certain circumstances to arise and keeps us from being tempted. Or, He may pull us through those temptations. We need to pray that God will "not lead us into temptation" (Matt. 6:13). On the other hand, God also allows us to fall into sin. He takes the restraints off and we give in to temptation. He gives us over to sin (Rom. 1:24, 26, 28). He lets whole nations go their own way into heinous sin (Acts 14:16). He lets go and we fall into sin under our own weight (Ps. 81:11–12; Acts 7:42). We ought to pray that God restrains sin in us.

10. God works miracles.

Most of what we have said so far has reference to God's general method of providence. Though still somewhat mysterious, there is a certain order to it. It is *usual providence*. But there is also *unusual providence*, in which

God acts in a special way. In general providence, He acts indirectly. Here He acts directly. A miracle is not just an unlikely event. It is one that goes contrary to the laws of nature. But God is free to suspend those laws, for after all it is He that is at work in all things anyway. Miracles are relatively rare. God alone can work miracles. They are signs that God is God. Jesus was God and did many miracles to prove it (John 20:30–31). The two greatest miracles regarding Christ were the virgin birth and the resurrection. Since then, the greatest miracle is the new birth and spiritual resurrection.

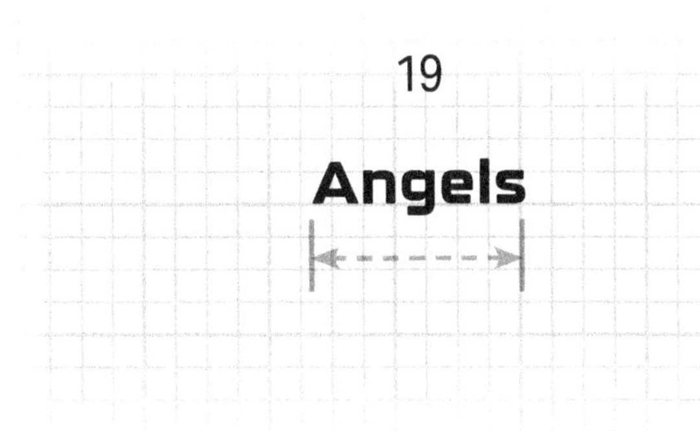

19 Angels

1. Angels are real.

Angels are real beings. They are not myths. They are not the product of overactive imaginations, hallucinations, mistaken identities, or hoaxes. They are not fairies, genies, or pixies. They are as real as human beings. They are not ghosts or the spirits of dead people. They were created by God before He created man, and they are higher than man (more intelligent, stronger, older, never sleep, etc.).

2. Angels are spirits.

Angels are frequently called "spirits" (Heb. 1:14). They do not have material, physical bodies as we do (Luke 24:39). They live in the heavenly realm but interact with us in the physical realm. They are invisible except for the rare times when God has let them become visible. They are personal. They have minds, memories, emotions, wills, consciences, morality, movement, and can talk. Unlike man, their number is limited, for God is not creating any more of them, nor do they marry and reproduce (Mark 12:25). Though it is not stated that angels are made in the image of God, in a sense they resemble God more than man does (like God, they are nonphysical, holy, etc.).

3. Angels are holy.

Scripture frequently describes them as "holy angels" (Mark 8:38; Rev. 14:10). It would seem that one third of the original angels fell into sin, leaving two-thirds as holy (Rev. 12:4). They never sinned and never will sin. Though they are moral beings with the capacity to sin, they never will fall. They always obey God (Ps. 103:20). Indeed, it is their highest delight to obey whatever God commands. This is what we should pray in the Lord's Prayer: "Your will be done on earth as it is in Heaven" (Matt. 6:10). These holy angels are elect (1 Tim. 5:21).

4. Angels are messengers of God.

The word *angel* in both Hebrew and Greek means "messenger, representative, one who runs an errand." They speak on God's behalf. On some occasions, they worked miracles. They seem to have a place in the affairs of the universe in a variety of ways, such as involvement with the planets. They take orders from God alone. We cannot command them, nor even speak to them, let alone pray to them (for prayer is a form of worship). The Old Testament sometimes speaks of a special messenger as "the Angel of the Lord," such as in Exodus 3:2. Many believers identify Him as the preincarnate, uncreated Lord Jesus Christ—God Himself bringing the message.

5. Angels worship God.

Among the many duties of the holy angels is worship. Most of the glimpses into Heaven recorded in Scripture reveal the presence of angels involved in worship. Specifically, Isaiah 6:3 and Revelation 4:8 describe how they sing and chant and fall down before the throne of

God, saying, "Holy, holy, holy." They directly see God in His glory and reflect this glory back to Him. Though they are also given sight into what's happening here in the physical part of the universe, their main activity is that of worship. They are commanded to worship God, and they most willingly and swiftly obey (Ps. 29:1–2; 103:20–21; 148:1–2). They worshiped Jesus at His birth (Heb. 1:6; Luke 2:9–14). We are forbidden to worship the angels (Col. 2:18; Rev. 22:8–9). One day, believers will join angels in the worship of God, but we will have a song to sing that even the angels cannot sing.

6. Angels have rank.

Angels are sometimes described as "the host of Heaven" (Gen. 2:1; Deut. 4:19; Jer. 33:22; etc.) God Himself is Lord Sabaoth, "the LORD of hosts" (Ps. 24:10). *Host* means a soldier in an army. The holy angels are God's heavenly army in the war against Satan's army of fallen angels. Thus, they have ranks. Scripture describes these as principalities, powers, rulers, thrones, etc. (Eph. 1:20; 6:12; Col. 1:16; 1 Peter 3:22; Rom. 8:38). The Bible also describes some angels as "cherubim" (Gen. 3:24) and others as "seraphim," or burning ones (Isa. 6:2).

7. Angels oppose demons.

There is a war going on in the supernatural realm between the good angels and the evil angels. Revelation 12 and parts of Daniel describe it, and a few other places give brief clues as to what is going on. Michael the archangel is the highest-ranking angel on one side, Satan on the other (Jude 9). *Archangel* means "chief angel." Christians and non-Christians are also involved in this spiritual war, but we do not see it as clearly as the angels do. While some popular writers have exaggerated and sensationalized this spiritual conflict, we should not ignore or trivialize it. It is real.

8. Angels are powerful.

They are called "mighty ones" (Ps. 29:1) and "powerful angels" (2 Thess. 1:7 NIV). They are more powerful than we are. Two of them blinded all the homosexuals in Sodom and Gomorrah (Gen. 19:11). One angel slew 185,000 Syrians in a single night (2 Kings 19:35). They are not omnipotent nor omnipresent nor omniscient. But they are more powerful than we are. The fallen angels lost their holiness but not their power, at least not all of it.

9. Angels serve Christians.

Hebrews 1:14 says of the good angels, "Are they not all ministering spirits sent forth to minister for those who will inherit salvation?" Several verses in Scripture indicate that there are indeed "guardian angels," though it is difficult to say if this means that each Christian has one specific angel or many, whether they come and go, etc. Psalm 91:11–12 is perhaps the clearest text that speaks of this work of the angels. Angels also escort us to Heaven when we die (Luke 16:22). They will be sent by Christ at the Rapture to escort us to be with Him without dying (Matt. 24:31; 1 Thess. 4:16). Meanwhile, they protect us from seen and unseen dangers, such as from demons.

10. Angels serve Christ.

The good angels serve our Lord Jesus in a variety of ways. First, since He is God, they take orders from Him and worship Him. When He was here on earth, the angels served Him in several ways. They ministered to Christ after the forty days in the wilderness, probably bringing Him food and water (Mark 1:13). When Christ was in the agony of sweating blood in Gethsemane, an angel appeared and strengthened Him (Luke 22:43). Christ told His captors that He had authority to call down thousands of angels to rescue Him (Matt. 26:53). Christ is not an angel but is their Commander-in-Chief, even higher than Michael. He is higher than the holy angels and is their Head (Col. 1:16; 2:10; Eph. 1:20–21; 1 Peter 3:22). He is not their mediator, per se, so far as salvation is concerned, for they do not need salvation. And though the angels are higher than we are, we will be elevated higher than the holy angels. They are the servants of the King of Kings, but we will be the bride.

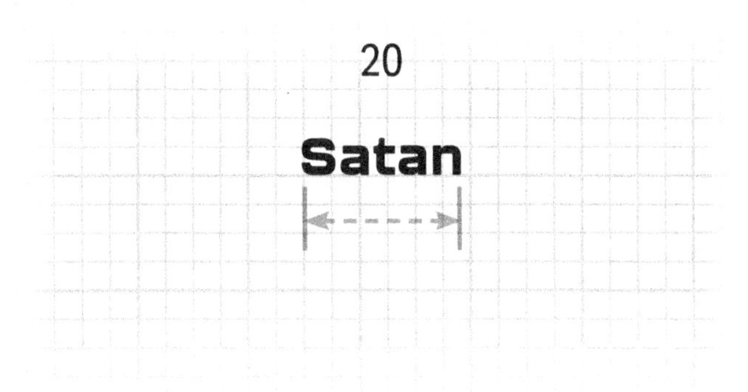

1. Demons are fallen angels.

Demons are real. They are not the product of superstition or fanciful imaginations. They are not goblins, ghouls, ogres, or banshees. Nor are they the ghosts of dead people come back to haunt us. They are angels who sinned and were expelled from Heaven. Revelation 12:4 indicates that about a third of the angels fell. Some are roaming around earth invisibly, others are kept in chains in a part of Hades called Tartarus to await their final judgment (2 Peter 2:4; Jude 6). There are many demons, but only one devil.

2. Demons are evil.

They are frequently called "unclean spirits" (Matt. 10:1), in contrast to the unfallen angels who are called "holy angels." They are "deceiving spirits" (1 Tim. 4:1). They are far more evil than humans, for they fell from a higher estate and have had more time to accumulate sins and stew in their evil. They know that God exists (James 2:19), but they refuse to obey Him. Yet they submit to God when He stretches forth His authority. Demons are involved in all areas of evil in the world. For example, they are the true identity of the false gods of pagan religions (1 Cor. 10:20).

3. Demons sometimes inhabit people.

The word usually translated "demon possessed" is literally *demonized*. Though all sinners are born as slaves to Satan, there is a sense in which demons indwell only some of them. Demon possession is relatively rare. It is not the same thing as disease, epilepsy, mental illness, or other afflictions, though sometimes demons are involved in these. The most evil and influential people in history (Hitler, Muhammad, mass murderers, etc.) were probably demon possessed. In demonization, two spirits indwell one body—a human and a demon. It probably begins with deep involvement in the occult. The only cure is exorcism by the authority of Jesus Christ.

4. Satan is real.

Satan is also very real. He was not invented to scare little children. Nor is he the projection or personification of our nightmares and evil ideas. He is not a myth. He has several names and titles: the devil (Matt. 4:1), the serpent (Gen. 3:1), Beelzebub (Matt. 12:24), Belial (2 Cor. 6:15), the dragon (Rev. 20:2), Abaddon and Apollyon (Rev. 9:11), and many others. Like the other angels, he was created before man. He is called the god of this world because he has been allowed to exercise a degree of control over mankind through sin (2 Cor. 4:4). He has a kingdom, inhabited by the whole world until a person escapes his clutches through salvation (1 John 5:19; Col. 1:13).

5. Satan was once a good archangel.

The original creation and fall of Satan are recorded somewhat mysteriously in Isaiah 14:12–17 and Ezekiel

28:12–19. The preceding verses rebuke men, but the following verses could not refer to mere men but to Satan behind them. Satan was an archangel, evidently named Lucifer, or light-bearer. He was the first created being to sin and led others into sin (Rev. 12:3–4). He wanted to become God, perhaps to stage a revolution. He was filled with pride (1 Tim. 3:6). Jesus saw him fall from Heaven like lightning (Luke 10:18). He is called the prince of demons (Matt. 12:24 NIV), for he led them into revolt and is still their leader.

6. Satan is evil.

One of the names for Satan is “the evil one” (Matt. 6:13). He is also “the wicked one” (1 John 5:19). He is the Prince of Darkness. He was the first one to sin and is the worst sinner in history. He is behind every evil thought, word, and deed. He has sinned longer and deeper than anyone else. The extent of his evil is almost inconceivable to us. Humans are totally depraved, that is, sin fills their entire beings. But Satan has a larger capacity to sin. Yet he is not infinitely evil, for only God is infinite in any way. Satan is not the equal opposite of God. The universe is a battlefield, but not between equals. Satan is vastly smaller than God. It would seem that his equal counterpart is Michael (Jude 9).

7. Satan tempts people to sin.

Just as Satan led other angels into sin, so he leads people into sin. In a way, he already has them, since they are born in sin. Still, he wants to keep them. He does not relinquish any without a fight. He wants to multiply sin in the universe. He is called “the tempter” (1 Thess. 3:5). He tempted Adam and Eve in the garden and tempted Jesus in the wilderness. He tempts us anywhere and everywhere. He advertises sin, makes it look desirable, and entices us to commit sin. One of the major means he uses is the sin that is already inside us (James 1:14). God Himself tempts no one but allows Satan to tempt us (James 1:13). That is how God tests us.

8. Satan disguises himself.

Satan rarely, if ever, reveals his evil designs and real motives. He disguised himself as a snake in the garden of Eden (Gen. 3:1). He pretends to offer good things to us. He is a deceiver. Jesus called him "a liar and the father of [lies]" (John 8:44). He cheats people in all sorts of ways. He lulls people into a sense of security, trapping them into ignoring their fate after death. Second Corinthians 11:13–15 says that he disguises himself as an "angel of light" and sends false prophets as spies in disguise to masquerade as ambassadors of truth. We need to beware of Satan's methods.

9. Satan accuses believers.

After he leads people into sin, he accuses them. Some of the accusations are true—they did sin. He uses this as an opportunity to kick fallen Christians and to try to keep them from getting up. He also accuses us falsely. Satan is "the accuser of our brethren, who accused them before our God day and night" (Rev. 12:10). He accused Job before God (Job 1), accused God before Adam and Eve (Gen. 3), and accused the God-man to His face (Matt. 4). Zechariah 3:1–5 is a good example of how Satan accuses people, but the righteousness of Christ defends them from all accusation. Christ is our advocate to defend us from Satan's accusations (Rom. 8:33–34).

10. Satan and demons will be punished in Hell.

Satan is under God's sovereign control. God lets him out and pulls him back as He pleases (Job 1 and 2). Christ defeated Satan and the demons at the cross. His death took away the power of Satan, who had the keys of death (Col. 2:15; Heb. 2:14; 1 John 3:8). Christ overthrew the Prince of Darkness and is bringing in the kingdom of light. One day Christ will return and will finish the job. Satan will be vanquished. He will be thrown into the pit of Hell for one thousand years, let out briefly, then thrown into the lake of fire forever (Rev. 20:1–3, 7–10). Hell was originally prepared as the final place of punishment for Satan and the demons (Matt. 25:41). There is no hope for Satan. He knows his time is short (Rev. 12:12). Neither Satan nor the demons were elect (1 Tim. 5:21). Christ did not die for them, nor is the gospel preached to them. Christ Himself will preside at their execution.

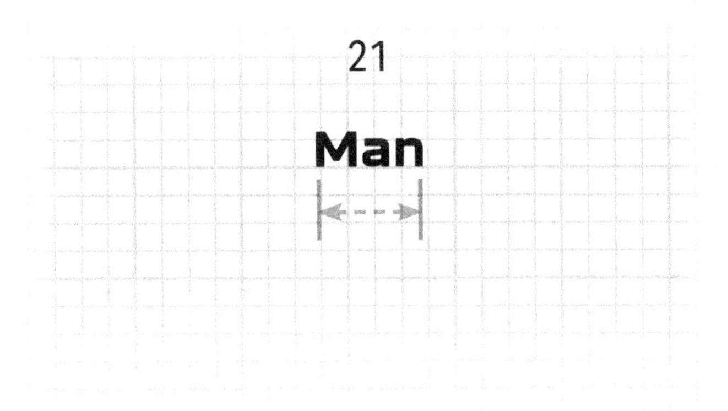

1. Man bears the image of God.

Man is man and God is God, and the twain never meet except in Christ the God-man. Nevertheless, man is like God in some respects. God made us in His image (Gen. 1:26–27). We can know God and have a loving relationship with Him. The image was marred but not destroyed by the fall. Because man still bears the image of God, we may not murder or curse our fellow man, for that would be an attack of God's image (Gen. 9:6; James 3:9). One day, the image will be restored to its pristine beauty in Christ (Rom. 8:29).

2. Man is not an animal.

Man did not evolve from the animals but was created higher than animals and lower than angels (Ps. 8:5). Man has some things in common with both but is neither an animal nor an angel. Like the animals, man has a physical body, has instinct, is affected by sin, etc. Like the angels and unlike the animals, man has a mind, a soul, a heart that can love, a conscience that tells him right and wrong, and a will that is subject to sin. Man has dominion over the animals and is not to treat his fellow man as an animal. And no animal or angel will ever be part of the bride of Christ.

3. Man is accountable to God.

God created us in a relationship of responsibility. We are accountable to God and will have to answer to Him one day (Rom. 14:12). We are culpable and guilty. We have the duty to fear and obey God (Eccl. 12:14). God holds us all liable for what we are, all we think, whatever we say, and everything we do. Man is subject to the law of God and is more accountable according to how much more light he has been given (Luke 12:48). All are accountable; some are more accountable and guiltier. We will all one day face God in court.

4. Man has a conscience.

God has put a certain mysterious quality within all of us that reminds us we will have to account to God. It is called a *conscience*. Romans 2 is the clearest passage on the subject. It is the echo of the voice of God, as it were. It is not audible, nor a perfect guideline. Some people's consciences are hardened and very indistinct (1 Tim. 4:2). Conscience both accuses and excuses, but mainly accuses. It troubles us (1 Sam. 24:5; 1 John 3:20). It is like an alarm telling us we are guilty.

5. Man is religious.

God created man to worship Him, and therefore gave man the capability to worship. Man is necessarily religious. He is a worshiping being. The trouble is, he worships the wrong thing. Instead of worshiping the true God, man worships idols. John Calvin said that each man's heart is an idol factory. This is why there are so many false religions. All men worship something or somebody. Man is *homo religioso*—religious man. The need to worship is as much a part of Him as his own shadow. To be precise, it is part of the image of God. The image of God is meant to lead us to worship God, for we were created to resemble God so that we might know Him, love Him, and worship Him. But because of sin, we love sin itself and will not worship the true God. Even the atheist has a religion known as *humanism*, the worship of man. It is self-worship. It takes other less obvious forms. Even pagan religions are forms of this, for in them fallen man creates his own false god in the image of man. What a distortion of the image of God! The image was meant to be a mirror to point us to worship our Creator, but we distort it so that our false god becomes a reflection of our own selves. Man is religious, but he follows a false religion.

6. Man is a dichotomy.

Does man have two or three basic components? Arguing from passages like 1 Thessalonians 5:23, some feel man has three parts (body, soul, spirit), each of which is quite different from the other. This tends to lead to mysticism, for it puts the mind in the soul and urges us to bypass it and use the spirit. Most orthodox Christians believe that man is a dichotomy, not a trichotomy. Man has a physical side and a spiritual side. The spiritual side has various aspects, which are not parts as such but various aspects of what Paul calls "the inner man" (Eph. 3:16) as opposed to our physical "outward man" (2 Cor. 4:16). First Thessalonians 5:23 no more teaches that man is three than Mark 12:30 teaches that man is four. Soul and spirit are somewhat synonymous (see Luke 1:46–47). Sometimes the *soul* refers to man in relation with man, and *spirit* to man in relation with God.

7. Man has a body.

Like the animals, man has a physical body. It has senses (sight, hearing, feel, smell, taste). It moves, grows, feels pain and pleasure, reproduces itself, etc. It was perfect in Eden, but is now mortal due to sin, and will be made immortal at our resurrection (1 Cor. 15). It is either male or female. One important part of the body is the blood, for in it is the very essence of physical life (Lev. 17:11, 14). Death comes when our spirit leaves our body (James 2:26). Men can kill the body, but only God can kill both body and soul in eternal Hell (Matt. 10:28). Our bodies belong to God (Rom. 12:1; 1 Cor. 6:19–20).

8. Man has a mind.

Man has a mind. The Greek word is *nous*. With our minds, we are able to think and reason. We can analyze, cogitate, compare. We use it to learn, gather information, store facts in our memory. Man's mind, however, is not a blank tablet. God has put within a part of our minds the knowledge that He exists (Rom. 1–2). We all know that He exists. This is where the mind overlaps with our conscience. It is questionable that we have a so-called subconscious side of our minds, at least as Freud said. Still, our minds are sometimes more awake than at other times and are asleep at night. Our minds have a sense of time past and future, so we can remember and plan. We also use our minds to communicate thoughts with others, especially through the wonderful means called language, which is a sort of symbolic verbalization of thoughts. Animals do not do this. Our minds are affected by sin. We are to use our minds for God.

9. Man has emotions.

Man has the capacity to feel. This produces emotions. Sometimes this is merely an inner reaction to the stimuli of the body. Some emotions are primarily inner, others outer. Generally, our emotions are of two sorts: pleasure and pain. Pleasurable emotions include joy, peace, thrill, fun, satisfaction, exhilaration, delight. Painful emotions include grief, worry, fear, anguish, confusion, loneliness. These have been greatly affected by sin, and so Christians are not to trust their feelings. God acts upon the emotions through the conscience to produce conviction of sin and works in them through redemption to produce true spiritual emotions. In Heaven, there is only pleasure; in Hell, only pain.

10. Man has a will.

Deep within us is our heart. In some contexts, it is where we think (Prov. 23:7). In others, where we feel (Acts 2:37). In still others, where we decide (Rom. 10:10). We sometimes call the deciding aspect the "will." God calls on us to choose properly (Josh. 24:15; Deut. 30:19). Our deepest affections cause us to choose or reject. The order is this: our nature, our mind, our choice.

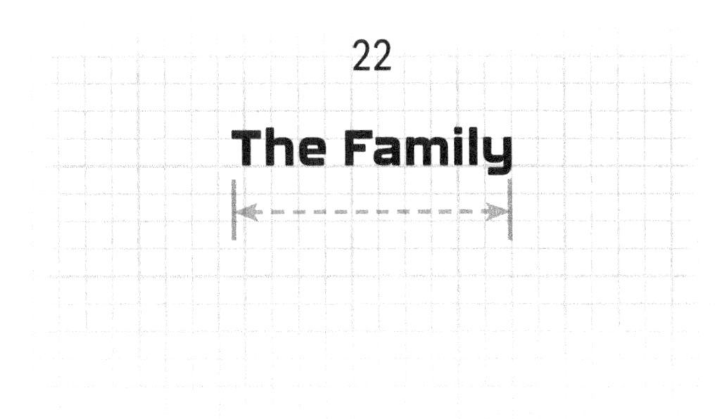

22

The Family

1. God created man as male and female.

God created Adam as the first man (1 Tim. 2:13). Out of one of his ribs, God created Eve, the first woman (Gen. 2:22). There are thus only two sexes. It is unnatural and ungodly to suggest a third or fourth, such as in homosexuality (a female man) and lesbianism (a male woman). The Bible forbids both male and female homosexuality, same-sex attraction, bisexuality and transgenderism. God considers them "an abomination" (Lev. 18:22) and "vile, . . . against nature, . . . shameful" (Rom. 1:26-27). God also created man and woman to be different in several ways, reflecting the roles God has for each. Men are stronger, more aggressive, more analytical, braver, abler to lead. Women are weaker, more protective, more intuitive and instinctive, and better able to nurture.

2. Adam and Eve were the first two humans.

Genesis 1 and 2 clearly teaches that Adam and Eve were individuals, not mere half-animal Neanderthals. Nor was there any kind of "pre-Adamic race," as suggested by weird esoteric theories, as in some extreme forms of the gap theory. The first man was every bit as human as any man today. This is more important than some evangelicals think. Deny it and the arguments in Romans 5, 1 Corinthians 15 and 1 Timothy 2 collapse.

3. All men are descended from Adam.

Adam was the father of all mankind. All were "in Adam" (1 Cor. 15:22). Even Eve was taken out of him. This is denied by evolutionists, who say we came from all sorts of half-humans in several places. Acts 17:26 says God made all peoples everywhere from this one man and we share the same life-giving essence of blood. We are all related to each other. Though there are differences of race, language, intellect, customs, and history, we all have more in common than we have in distinction. We were in Adam physically, in that his seed reproduced descendants. Adam was also our *federal head*, or representative in Eden. When he fell, we fell (Rom. 5:12). We inherit both his human nature and his sin (Eph. 2:3).

4. God ordained marriage.

God created Eve out of Adam to reunite them in the special bond of matrimony. It was God's idea, not Adam's. Genesis 2 shows the main reasons for marriage then and now: companionship, to reproduce the race, to serve God better in the work God gives, and to serve as an example of spiritual relationship with God. Marriage is a creation ordinance and so is applicable to all men, not just Christians. God's rule is one man, one woman, one lifetime. God does not permit polygamy, incest, homosexuality, and other such things. Though most people do marry, it is optional (1 Cor. 7). God wrote the basic laws for marriage in nature and more explicitly in the Bible. It works when done right, fails when done wrong.

5. God commands husbands to love their wives.

There are several important rules and principles that God has laid down for marriage. One is that couples must follow God's Word. Another is that they are to serve and love Him first and foremost. God has also given specific rules for husbands and wives relative to their roles. They are all summed up in one rule for each. The main duty of a husband is: "Husbands, love your wives" (Eph. 5:25; Col. 3:19; see also 1 Peter 3:7). He is to sacrifice his wants for her needs, even willing to die for her as Christ died for the church. He is to protect and provide for her, lead her, be gentle and courageous, and cherish and nourish her. He should imitate Christ in His dealings with the church, not imitate the views of the world. God has fitted men for this, and it is their prime duty.

6. God commands wives to submit to their husbands.

The major duty of wives is: "Wives, submit to your own husbands, as to the Lord" (Eph. 5:22; see also Col. 3:18, 1 Peter 3:1–6). She is to obey him, respect him, follow his lead. She must submit to his authority when he exercises it within the God-ordained circle, and of course, she must not follow him if he goes outside that boundary. Marriage is thus a hierarchy of rank, not an egalitarian democracy. The wife is also to learn from him in silence (1 Tim. 2:11–12). All this is very unpopular and quite politically incorrect, but it is right and true. Indeed, the success of a marriage can be measured by the extent to which both husbands and wives do their respective duties. All breakdowns in marriage can be traced back to either or both not doing what God tells them to do.

7. God commands couples to have children.

Genesis 1 and 2 explicitly state that one of the major reasons for marriage is the reproduction of humankind.

God forbids us to do it outside of marriage. Children are a blessing from the Lord (Ps. 127:3–5). God commands married couples to be fruitful and multiply (Gen. 1:28). Of course, God sometimes providentially withholds children from some couples (1 Sam. 1:5) for a variety of reasons (that they may serve him in a different way, for example). But the Bible does not permit us to make the choice by means of birth control. On the other hand, God does allow adoption, especially for couples who cannot have children by themselves. Finally, parents are to raise their children by the Bible, in the instruction of the Lord, with love and firmness, and with appropriate discipline and patience (Eph. 6:4).

8. God commands children to obey their parents.

The major duty of children is to obey their parents (Eph. 6:1). They do not have authority with or over their parents. God does not allow family voting, "kids' rights," or other such humanistic ungodliness. Parents must teach, children must learn. Parents must chasten, children must submit to it (Heb. 12:7–9). Children are under their parents' authority until they marry and leave the home, or until both parents die (Gen. 2:24; Ex. 20:12). If parents raise their children correctly, they instill in them lifelong habits and character (Prov. 22:6), though they cannot guarantee that they will be saved. If the children grow up wild and wicked, they have to answer to God—and so do the parents.

9. God allows for divorce on two grounds.

God ordained marriage, but He also permits divorce—but on only two grounds. He does not permit it for mental cruelty, spousal abuse, failure to financially support a family, or drunkenness (though these are sins that God does care about, and need to be dealt with and not allowed to continue), nor for incompatibility, lost affections, irreconcilable differences, and so on. The first ground is an unrepentant act of adultery (Matt. 5:32; 19:9). It must be an act, not merely a thought, a look, or a word. It would include homosexuality. It must also be unrepentant, for if the guilty party repents, the other must forgive (Eph. 4:32). Either party may divorce the other (Mark 10:11–12). The second ground is in 1 Corinthians 7:12–15. If a non-Christian deserts and divorces their Christian spouse, the Christian need not resist. It does not appear that the Christian can initiate this divorce, and this desertion ground does not apply except in a Christian/non-Christian marriage. A biblical divorce frees the innocent party to remarry.

10. The family is to serve God.

Let us not forget the main reason God ordained marriage and children: to serve God. God gave Eve to Adam to help him serve in the garden (Gen. 2:18). Families must serve God together in church and in the specific ministry that God has called them to. They form a team which can generally serve God better than they could as individuals. God blesses and uses families who follow His directions. And Satan hates and wishes to destroy them.

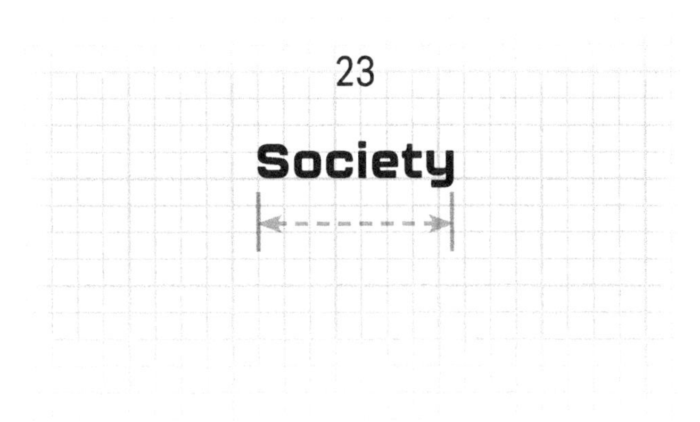

1. All aspects of human society are to be under God.

"One nation under God" is a good biblical motto (Ps. 33:12). Individuals are under God's rule, and so are all relationships between individuals (families, government, employment, churches, etc.). Indeed, all aspects of society are also to be submitted to God's rule for God's glory. This would include work, entertainment, business, education, art, communication, literature, science, and many others. This is part of the cultural mandate God gave to Adam in Genesis 1:28. The great Abraham Kuyper, a Calvinist theologian who became prime minister of Holland, said, "There is not one square inch in the universe of which Christ does not say, 'Mine'."

2. God commands man to work.

Part of this cultural mandate is the command to work. Note that God gave this work order to Adam before the fall (Gen. 1:28; 2:15). He was to till the garden. After the fall, God did not annul this order, but made it harder. The curse of sin means that we must sweat and toil to do our work (Gen. 3:17–19). It is a life sentence of hard labor. Eve was to help him (Gen. 2:18), and today both individuals and couples are to work to use the creation to glorify God. The husband's main place is outside the home, the wife's in the home (Titus 2:5). We are to rest one day, but that means we are to work the other six (Ex. 20:9). Laziness is frequently condemned in Scripture (Prov. 6:6, 9). God blesses us in several ways for good work, such as the satisfaction that comes from a job well done (Eccl. 5:18). The early Protestants, especially the Calvinists, developed what is termed the *Protestant work ethic*, which is the basis for the modern free enterprise system. It involves the principles of hard work, thrift, reinvestment, honest dealings, and generous charity to those in need (Eph. 4:28).

3. God ordained private property.

"You shall not steal" means that some things belong to some people and not to others (Ex. 20:15). All things belong to God, but He has given them to people by way of delegated stewardship. Theft is wrong (robbery, burglary, wrongful lawsuits, deceptive advertising, etc.). But extortionate taxation is also a form of stealing, for the Bible teaches Christian capitalism, not socialism. We are to use our belongings by the rules of the Bible, both individually and collectively in our dealings with others.

4. God created human government.

Just as God ordained the family and the church, so God also ordained the state. Romans 13 is the main passage on this. Rulers are ordained by God. God raises them up and brings them down (Luke 1:52). He uses even ungodly rulers to carry out His purposes (Prov. 21:1). Government was not man's idea, and today it is not left to man to think up what is the best kind of government. God has told us the general outline for all governments to follow.

5. Israel was meant to serve as a model society.

One of the reasons God raised up Israel as a nation was for it to serve as a model society. On the one hand, it was given certain laws and blessings that were not applicable to Gentile nations. For instance, Israel alone was given a direct and explicit land grant. On the other hand, in other ways Israel was to be a model society. The ideal was not for a monarchy, but for a theocracy (1 Sam. 8:4–7). This applies to Gentiles in that they must submit their government and society to God. Judges, not kings, are closer to the ideal. There is no direct theocracy outside of Israel. But even today, we can learn much from its laws and system—and from its mistakes.

6. Government should be righteous.

God holds all individuals responsible to obey Him—He also holds all governments and persons in authority responsible. God judged gentile nations in the Old Testament for failure to obey Him, and He still does. Think of Sodom and Gomorrah, Egypt, Assyria, Babylon, and Rome. The standard of righteousness is not majority opinion, advice from the intellectual elite, whatever is new, or other concoctions of man. Rather, it is the Bible. Rulers cannot guarantee the salvation of its people, any more than parents can their children. But they can punish evildoers and reward good doers (Rom. 13:3–4), and thus instill a kind of national character. God has two kingdoms, as it were: the state and the church. Both are under God. One has the sword, the other the Word. They are related, but not identical. But both are under God and should follow the Bible.

7. Christians ought to be good citizens.

Just as Adam was to work in the garden for God's glory, so Christians are to be involved in all aspects of society to God's glory, including the state. Christians may vote, serve on juries, join the military, serve as elected and appointed officials, etc. They should analyze the nature of their government and compare it to God's ideal in Scripture, then act wisely to help bring it into conformity with God's Word. Naturally this is difficult. We are to be good citizens, and God uses our presence to influence the world, restrain sin, prepare for the spread of the gospel, bless families, and so forth.

8. God condemns both tyranny and anarchy.

God's ideal is the "Righteous Republic" of judges, not kings. Democracy is similar but is rooted in Greek philosophy rather than biblical revelation. Tyranny is the idea that one man at the top is the law. He himself is above the law. We see this in Nazism, Caesarism, Pharaohism, and Communism. Even some of Israel's kings became dictators. A monarchy is better but can be good or bad. Saul was a poor king; David, a good one. There is no "divine right of kings" in the Bible. That was invented by medieval kings working with the papacy to reinforce their authority. On the other hand, God does not approve of pure democracy, libertarianism, or outright anarchy. In a way, the worst government is better than no government. Israel swung to both extremes in the book of Judges.

9. God ordained the sword.

God gave the sword to the state (Rom. 13:4) and in a lesser way to individuals. The church has the power of the Word to convert, not the sword to punish. The state can and must use force to punish and protect. This principle means that the state may wage just war (Deut. 20), execute criminals (Num. 35), arm the police, and so on. Individuals have a limited use of the sword (Luke 22:36), but this does not allow for vigilantism or personal revenge. God ordained the police and the military, as well as judges and elected officials. They must use the sword as God ordains.

10. No human government will ever be perfect.

We should pray for our leaders (1 Tim. 2:1–2) and be like salt and light in society (Matt. 5:13–16). We can effect much good. We should obey the cultural mandate as well as the Great Commission. Yet, for all our efforts, there will never be the perfect society until Christ returns. Men are still sinners. Even on an island populated by Christians, we still have sin—and a new generation always replaces us. Most societies and governments have been very evil and corrupt, unjust, and wicked, adding to man's sin and misery. This is not an excuse to hide, but an incentive to work, pray, and evangelize until Christ returns and sets up His kingdom.

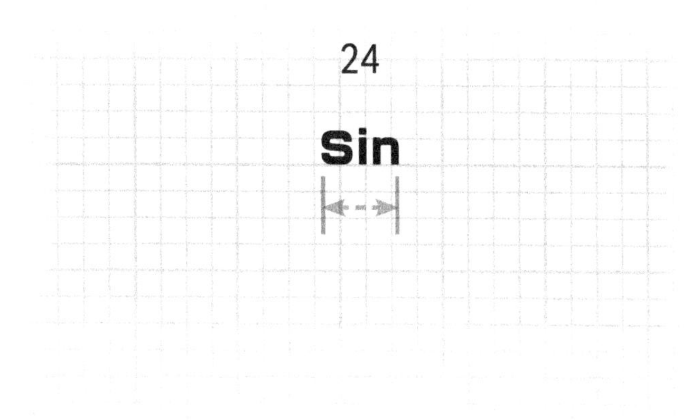

24

Sin

1. God permitted the existence of sin.

God predestined and foreordained everything that will ever happen (Rom. 11:36). Therefore, God predestined sin. Sin is not an accident; it is part of God's overall plan to glorify Himself. God foreordained sin so as to further glorify His holiness and love. God is glorified in His wrath by punishing sin and in His grace by forgiving it (Rom. 9:22–23). The first one to sin was Satan, but that was not the actual beginning. It was planned. God predestined it negatively and by permission, rather than positively and actively, as He did in predestinating good.

2. God cannot be blamed for sin.

Though God predestined its existence, God cannot be blamed or accused. In this sense, God is not the author of sin, nor its approver, essential source, or promoter. God is holy. He does only that which is holy. God does no evil or wickedness. Nor does He tempt people to sin (James 1:13). This is a deep mystery. But it is sufficient for us to remember Romans 9:19–20. Sinful man cannot blame the sinless God. The faultfinder is at fault and cannot find fault in God (Ezek. 18:25; Job 40:2).

3. God put Adam and Eve in a covenant of works.

Adam and Eve were created holy and innocent, not neutral. But it was a kind of naive innocence; it needed to be tested. So God put them on a conditional standing. If they obeyed, they would be granted immortality. Otherwise, they would die (Gen. 2:16–17). We call this the *covenant of works*. They did not earn or merit salvation. Rather, they were tested to see if they would maintain their loyalty to God. Adam was the federal head, or representative, for all mankind. If he passed, they passed; if he failed, they failed. Some think the test was for a short probationary time; others say it was perpetual. Either way, it was conditional.

4. Adam and Eve disobeyed God.

They failed the test and broke the covenant of works. It took only a single act of disobedience. This was the first sin on earth, and through it sin and death entered to the rest of humanity (Rom. 5:12). Eve was the first one to sin, and unlike Adam, she was deceived, while Adam went into it deliberately (1 Tim. 2:14). Their sin involved more than eating the forbidden fruit, whatever it was. It included unbelief in God's word, making themselves the test of all truth, obedience to Satan, idolatry, selfishness, greed, putting tangible pleasures before spiritual duties, disregard for the glory of God, and many other sins. They were punished with immediate spiritual death, eventual physical death, banishment from Eden, and loss of fellowship with God. Adam was cursed with having to sweat hard in his work, and Eve was cursed with labor pains in childbirth and the tendency to rebel against Adam (Gen. 3:16–19).

5. Sin is lawlessness and disobedience to God's law.

The Bible, not psychology or majority opinion, determines what sin is. God defines sin as the breaking of

His law (1 John 3:4). God's law is summed up in the two love commandments (Matt. 22:37–40) and in the Ten Commandments (Ex. 20:1–17). Sin is when we fail to do what God tells us to do or when we do what God tells us not to do. We call these sins of *omission* and *commission* (see James 4:17). One word for sin means failure to hit the mark. A *trespass* is when we do what we ought not to do, like trespassing where we ought not to go. A *transgression* is an act of disobedience to a known law. An *iniquity* is an inequality in our dealings with God and man.

6. There are many kinds of sins.

There are many catalogs of sins in the Bible and also many examples. There are also various kinds of sins. Some sins involve the body, others the mind (Eph. 2:3). Some are internal only, others involve external acts. We sin in thought, word, and deed. Some sins are new, others old. Some are habits or besetting sins (Heb. 12:1). We are born in original sin and later commit individual acts of actual sin. Some sins are civil crimes, others not. Some are against ourselves (vice), others are against other people. Some are mortal, others non-mortal (1 John 5:16–17) The list goes on and on. But all are evil, wicked, black, and despicable.

7. Some sins are worse than others.

All sins deserve punishment, but some deserve more punishment than others. Some are crimes which deserve punishment here on earth, either by civil law or by God's direct act. Judas had a "greater sin" than Pilate (John 19:11). Sin is determined by knowledge of God's law, and some have the law only in conscience and nature, while others have it in the Bible (Rom. 2:14–15). A willful and deliberate sin is worse than a sin of ignorance (Num. 15:22–31). An external sin is worse than one which is only internal, for it involves both. A repeated sin is worse than a new sin. Sins directly against God (such as blasphemy or sacrilege) are worse than those directly against man (such as envy). Murder is worse than hate. Some deserve more punishment in Hell than others (Luke 12:47–48). But even the smallest sin is far worse than we think.

8. There is an unpardonable sin.

Unless a person is forgiven, he will be punished in Hell. But there is a unique kind of sin mentioned in Matthew 12:31–32 that is unpardonable both in this life and in the next. It is the blasphemy against the Holy Spirit. It is very rare and confirms that a person is reprobate and will never repent. A person commits it when he is convinced that the special work of God is real, but he attributes it to Satan rather than to God. This is similar to the extreme form of apostasy in Hebrews 6. Apostasy is when a person renounces his profession of faith in Christ and the gospel, showing that he never was truly saved to begin with. In some cases, this involves the unpardonable blasphemy against the Holy Spirit.

9. There is no excuse for sin.

Adam blamed Eve; Eve blamed Satan (Gen. 3:12). Adam blamed Eve and God (Gen. 3:13). We try to shift the blame onto others, such as friends and family, our environment, etc. But we can blame no one but ourselves. We cannot blame Adam for original sin, for we were part of Adam. We cannot say, "Someone tempted me," like Eve did, nor "I couldn't help it." Nor can we blame God in any way. Though God foreordained sin, we alone have the guilt. God tests us by allowing us to be tempted by Satan, but He Himself does not solicit to sin (James 1:13). Indeed, God always provides a way of escape from temptation if we would only listen (1 Cor.

10:13). Sin is no small thing. It is no laughing matter. Only fools scoff at sin or make excuses (Prov. 14:9).

10. Sinners deserve punishment.

Sin brings guilt. We are responsible to God and culpable for our every thought, word, and deed. Every person deserves to be punished. God is angry with all sinners (Ps. 7:11) and everyone deserves to be punished in Hell forever, no matter how many sins they have committed or of what kind. Romans 6:23 says, "The wages of sin is death," meaning, we have earned it. The thief on the cross spoke rightly when he said, "We are getting what we deserve" (see Luke 23:40–41). In repentance, we admit that we have no excuse and have only ourselves to blame. Confession means we admit that we deserve to be punished in Hell. Conviction of sin is when we finally know it (John 16:8; Ps. 51:3).

25

The Consequences of Sin

1. All people inherit Adam's sin.

Romans 5 teaches the great doctrine known as *original sin*. It does not refer to the first or original sin of eating the forbidden fruit, but to how we were in Adam and have inherited sin. We were in Adam in essence and by representation. When he sinned, we sinned. When he sinned, his soul died and was thrown into a state of rebellion with God. We are born in that state. Ephesians 2:3 says we were all "by nature children of wrath." The image of God is defaced in our nature, but we bear a close resemblance to Adam (see Gen. 5:3). Original sin refers to our nature, what we are. Actual sins flow from it. We have the nature of sin and the necessity of sinning. It is as much a part of us as our fingerprints or DNA code.

2. We are born guilty.

Pelagians deny original sin. Semi-Pelagians and Arminians agree that we inherit something from Adam—they say we inherit the tendency to sin but not the sin itself and certainly not the guilt. The Bible teaches that we inherit the sin and the guilt. It is not that we are guilty of something we did not do. Rather, we were in Adam doing it, and he was our representative. We were born in sin, born evil by nature (Gen. 6:5; 8:21; Pss. 51:5; 58:3; Isa. 48:8; Prov. 22:15). And we are born guilty too, for how can there be sin without guilt? We were born sinful, guilty, condemned.

3. Dying infants go to Heaven.

Scripture seems to teach that all dying infants go to Heaven. This is apparent from passages like Matthew 19:14 and 2 Samuel 12:23 (David's dying baby) and so on. They died before the age of a formed consciousness (Isa. 7:15–16; Jon. 4:11), what some call the *age of accountability*. This does not mean they were innocent, however. Rather, it means that God has elected all dying infants to be saved. That they die proves they are guilty; that they are saved proves they are elect. They are incapable of faith, and their original sin deserves Hell. But God graciously saves them by grace, and they are given faith as they enter Heaven. Some evangelicals leave the question open or offer other opinions on the matter.

4. All have sinned.

Since all people are descended from Adam (Acts 17:26) and inherit his sin and guilt, it follows that all of them eventually commit individual acts of sin. There are many verses that teach that everyone everywhere has sinned against God, of which Romans 3:23 is the most well-known. There are no exceptions, except for the Lord Jesus Christ, who was not descended from Adam because of the virgin birth (Luke 1:35). Some sin more than others, but everyone is sinful and guilty before God. In fact, we were born in the state of sin and have never known innocence. Adam and Eve were the only two humans (except Christ) who ever knew what it was to be innocent, and their innocence was temporary.

5. Sin infects every part of our being.

We are all totally depraved. Sin affects and infects all persons and all parts of every person. Isaiah 1:5–6 compares us to a sick body which is infected by disease from head to toe. Sin indwells us in our body, mind, soul, heart, conscience, emotions, will, memory—down to the smallest part. A little leaven leavens the whole lump (1 Cor. 5:6). Calvinists alone teach this awesome doctrine. Arminians and others say that our minds or maybe our wills are not affected, or if affected are not totally affected. But the Bible is clear: we are a seething mass of sin.

6. Man is evil, not good.

To answer the old philosophical and religious question, "Is man basically good with some evil or evil with some good?" the Bible teaches something more drastic. Man is bad, bad, bad. Bad to the bone. Not even a little good is left in him. Romans 7:18, "in me . . . nothing good dwells." Jesus said in Matthew 7:11, "you then, being evil" and in verses 16–18 He added that we are like bad trees bearing bad fruit. Because of original sin, there is no good but only bad in us. Indeed, we are sons of the devil (John 8:44). The difference between us and Satan is quantitative, not qualitative.

7. Man does not have free will.

Man is responsible to obey God but is no longer able to do so. His will is dead and therefore incapable of doing what only a live will could do. We are born slaves to sin (John 8:34; Rom. 6:20; 2 Peter 2:19) and slaves of Satan (2 Tim. 2:26). We are willing slaves, too, who do not want to be free. We sin in order to assert our pretended freedom from God. Our wills are dead, not merely sick (Eph. 2:1, 5; Col. 2:13). If our will is so frequently said to be dead and a slave, how can anyone say it is alive and free?

8. Man is unable to obey God.

Fallen man does not have the ability anymore to obey God, or to believe, repent, love God, or anything else of virtue. This is the doctrine of *total inability*. We cannot come to Christ because we are bound in sin (John 6:44, 65). It is not that we want to but can't; rather, we cannot want to. Our natures and wills must be changed before we are able. Matthew 7:18, "A bad tree [cannot] bear good fruit." Romans 8:8, "Those who are in the flesh cannot please God." But this inability does not negate our responsibility. It does not lessen our guilt but compounds it.

9. Man loves sin and hates God.

Because of the extremely black state of man's heart in total depravity and inability, sin manifests itself in two basic ways. First, man loves sin. He is addicted to it and enjoys sin (Job 15:16). He loves sin as sin. This is not always conscious, but by nature and choice. Second, fallen man hates God. See John 3:19–20 and Matthew 6:24. No man is neutral to God; he is either for Him or against Him. The man in Adam is against God and for sin; the man in Christ is for God and against sin. Fallen men hate God and therefore also hated Christ (John 7:7; 15:18). They still do.

10. Man cannot save himself.

Some people don't know they are lost, and they don't care. Others sense they are lost and care enough to try to do something about it. They invent all sorts of religions, all false. Some try building bridges to God by their own good works, such as charity and philanthropy. Others try to keep the Golden Rule, the Sermon on the Mount, or the Ten Commandments. Still others think that they can be saved from the wrath of God against sin by being baptized, taking Communion, going to church, singing in the choir, reading their Bible, or putting money in the offering basket. These are good things, but none of them can save anyone. Why? Because no one can be saved by his good works (Rom. 3:28; Gal. 2:16; Eph. 2:8–9; Titus 3:5). For one thing, fallen man cannot even do a true good work. Even if he could, he could never do enough. We are not saved by having more good works than bad, as many think. Man can no more give himself life than a corpse can. He cannot earn salvation for himself, let alone for anyone else (Ps. 49:7). He cannot change his fallen nature (Jer. 13:23). He is dead, lost, doomed, damned, utterly without hope of himself (Eph. 2:1–3, 12). And unless God alone does something, he'll go to Hell.

26

The Person of Christ

1. Jesus was a real historical person.

Throughout Christ's ministry, people kept wondering who He was (Matt. 8:27). Jesus asked His own disciples and received various replies (Luke 9:18–20). Our eternal destiny hinges on what we believe about Jesus Christ. The first point is that Jesus was a real person. He lived at a certain time and place. History is measured BC ("before Christ") and AD ("*anno Domini*," "in the year of the Lord") around Him. He was not a myth and the gospel accounts of Him are true (Luke 1:1–4). Most liberals say that there are so many myths about Jesus in the New Testament that we can know only very little about the real Jesus. They say, "The Jesus of history is not the Christ of faith." They are wrong. We do not need to "demythologize" the biblical Jesus. We need to believe in Him as a real person exactly as recorded in God's infallible Word. Also, He was not a fairy tale, a hallucination, or other such nonsense.

2. Jesus is the center of God's dealings with man.

Colossians 1:18 says that "in all things He [has] the preeminence." He is the conduit through which God has all His dealings with man, yes, even the whole cosmos. God is revealed personally only through Jesus (John 1:18). God created the entire universe through Jesus (John 1:2–3). He is the means by which God reveals and receives glory (Heb. 1:1–3). This is a Christocentric universe. Christ is the apex, the hub, the center, the ultimate reference point in everything between God and us.

3. The name *Jesus* means "Jehovah saves."

When Jesus was about to be born, an angel told Joseph that He was to be named Jesus, "for He will save His people from their sins" (Matt. 1:21). In Greek, it is *Iesous*. In Hebrew, it is *Yeshua*, or Joshua. As pointed out in the book of Hebrews, Joshua took the Israelites into the promised land after Moses; so Jesus saves from sins which the law cannot save (Acts 13:39). Jesus is the Savior. He is God Himself coming in human flesh to save His people. God did not merely send a savior—He came as a Savior.

4. Jesus is the Messiah.

The angel gave Jesus a second name, *Emmanuel* ("God with us") (Matt. 1:23), which is similar to what we would consider a middle name. *Christ* is not His last name but the title of one of His offices. *Christ* in Greek is *Christos*. In Hebrew, it is *Masiach*, or Messiah. Both words mean "anointed one." Just as Old Testament prophets, priests, and kings were anointed with oil when they were ordained to their offices, so Jesus was anointed with the Holy Spirit in His ordination at His baptism (Matt. 3:16). This had to do with His office regarding His work, not His person. He was the Son of Abraham (the one who inherited the promises to Abraham, Gal. 3) and the Son of David (heir of Davidic throne, Ps. 89). He is Messiah for Jews and Gentiles.

5. Jesus fulfilled the prophecies of the Messiah.

Long before He was born, Jesus' coming had been predestined, promised, and predicted by God through His prophets. Genesis 3:15 was the first such prediction and in some ways is the most important. The Old Testament is filled with dozens of others, some clear (Ps. 22; Isa. 53), some not so clear. In a way, the whole Old Testament spoke about the coming Messiah (Luke 24:25–26, 44–46; Acts 10:43; 1 Cor. 15:3–4). The four Gospels, especially Matthew, point out how Jesus fulfilled them. Some are to be fulfilled at His second coming. These were irrefutable proofs that Jesus was who He claimed.

6. Jesus is the Great Prophet.

Moses predicted a prophet greater than himself would come one day—it was Jesus (Deut. 18:15–19; Acts 3:22). The prophets who were merely human said, "Thus says the Lord." Jesus said, "I say to you" (Matt. 5:22, 28, 32, 34, 39, 44). They said, "The word of the Lord came to me." Jesus is the Word of God come to us in person. He is called the *Logos* (Word) in John 1:1 and 14 and in Revelation 19:13. (See also 1 John 1:1). This refers not so much to the words which Jesus spoke, as to His very person and office as God's personal and highest revelation of Himself (Heb. 1:1–3). Some people then and now think Jesus was only a human prophet (Matt. 16:14). No. He was the Great Prophet. Muslims claim that Muhammad was the Prophet. They are sorely wrong.

7. Jesus is the Great High Priest.

Scripture often speaks of the three main offices of Christ: prophet, priest, and king. No one person in the Old Testament was ever all three, and Jesus is all three in a unique sense. In each, He is greater than those who came before Him: greater than priests (Matt. 12:6), greater than prophets (12:41), greater than kings (12:42). The book of Hebrews especially explains the high priestly work of Christ. He is greater than Melchizedek and Levi. He brought a greater sacrifice, typified by all the animal sacrifices. He Himself is the Lamb of God, the great and final sacrifice (John 1:29; Heb. 9:24–28). The great Shepherd-Priest became a lamb in order to sacrifice Himself.

8. Jesus is Lord.

The third major office is king, or Lord. He is the Lord Jesus Christ. He is Lord of Lords and King of Kings (Rev. 17:14; 19:16; 1 Tim. 6:15). He is the King of the Jews (Matt. 2:2) and the "ruler over the kings of the earth" (Rev. 1:5). He is Lord of All (Acts 10:36; Rom. 10:12). Over and over the New Testament states that "Jesus is Lord" (e.g., 1 Cor. 12:3). He is Lord in two ways. First, He is Lord by virtue of His eternal deity. Second, He is Lord by virtue of His becoming the God-man who humbled Himself to the lowest depths and was exalted to the highest heights (Phil. 2:5–11). He already is Lord now and will be recognized as such at the second coming and the last judgment, and forever by all.

9. Jesus is the *second Man* and *last Adam*.

Romans 5 and 1 Corinthians 15 speak of yet another related office of the Lord Jesus. He is the "second Man" and the "last Adam." Just as Adam was the father and federal head of a race of humanity, so the Lord Jesus is the father and federal head of a new race of humanity. This new race is not biologically new, but is taken out of the first race by election and salvation. Jesus succeeded where Adam failed.

10. Jesus is the only way to God.

Since He is what He is and occupies all these offices alone, especially as the unique conduit between God and man, it follows that Jesus is the only way to God. "I am the way, the truth, and the life. No one comes to the Father except through Me" (John 14:6). He is the only door (John 10:9). There is salvation in nobody else (Acts 4:12). He is the only mediator between God and man, for He alone is both God and man (1 Tim. 2:4). We will die in our sins unless we believe in the person of Jesus (John 8:24). But we will live in Him if we believe the truth about Him. Through Jesus alone can we know God (John 17:3), for Jesus alone knows God perfectly and personally, and it is He who determines who will be granted a personal introduction to His Father (Matt. 11:27).

27

The Deity of Christ

1. Jesus Christ is explicitly called God.

There are over one hundred proofs of the deity of Jesus Christ in the Bible. Several verses explicitly call Him God: John 1:1, "The Word was God"; John 20:28, "My Lord and my God"; 1 Timothy 3:16, "God was manifested in the flesh"; 2 Peter 1:1, "our God and Savior Jesus Christ"; Titus 2:13, "our great God and Savior Jesus Christ"; Matthew 1:23, "God with us"; 1 John 5:20 (ESV), "He is the true God"; Hebrews 1:8, "Your throne, O God, is forever and ever"; Isaiah 9:6, "Mighty God." Jesus Christ is one hundred percent God. He is not part God, a lesser god, or one of many gods. He is God.

2. Jesus said that He is God.

Each of the four Gospels records Christ's assertions of deity, but especially the Gospel of John. Note how often Jesus used the special name of Jehovah, "I Am," of Himself. Sometimes it was "I am the bread of life" (John 6:35); "I am the light of the world" (John 8:12); "I am the way, the truth, and the life" (John 14:6); etc. Sometimes it was simply "I AM" (John 8:24, 58). The Jews knew that He claimed to be God (John 5:18; 10:33). In the last book of the Bible, Jesus said, "I am the Alpha and the Omega, the Beginning and the End, the First and the Last" (Rev. 22:13; see also 1:8; 21:6). He was either a liar, a lunatic, or Lord. The truth is that He was exactly what He said He was.

3. Jesus did not become God.

The Bible clearly teaches that Jesus did not become God at a certain time but was God from all eternity. He is eternal and divine, for God alone is truly eternal (John 1:1; 8:58; 17:5; Col. 1:17; Isa. 9:6). He was not a man who somehow became God, as the Mormons and others teach. Rather, He was God who became a man.

4. Jesus is equal to the Father and the Holy Spirit.

John 1:1 says that Jesus "was with God, and . . . was God." This is the Trinity. He was God and with the other two members of the Trinity. All three are equally divine. His equality with them is taught in John 5:18 and 10:33 and especially in Philippians 2:6. Only God could be equal to God. Since there is only one God, this means the Trinity. Jesus has the same nature as the Father and the Spirit, not merely a similar nature, let alone a different nature. When He became a man, He humbled Himself, and in that state, He could say that the Father was greater than Himself (John 14:28). But that referred to the incarnation and the state of humiliation, not to His eternal essence as deity.

5. Jesus is omnipotent, omnipresent, and omniscient.

Jesus possessed the unique qualities of deity, such as these three attributes of God. No mere man or angel has ever or could ever possess any of them, and Jesus has all of them. He is omnipotent and can do all things, for He is "[God] Almighty" (Rev. 1:8; see also Isa. 9:6, "Mighty God"). His omnipotence is also taught in 2 Peter 1:16,

Philippians 3:21, and Matthew 8:27. Second, Jesus is omnipresent. He fills all things and is with His people everywhere (Eph. 1:23; 4:10; Matt. 18:20; 28:20). Thirdly, He is omniscient. He knows everything, even the secret thoughts of men (John 2:24–25; 4:29; 6:64; 16:30; 21:17). Furthermore, Jesus is also immutable, or unchangeable, in His deity (Heb. 1:12; 13:8). He did not cease to be God when He became a man, and His humanity does not possess these attributes of deity. But that He has them proves that He is God.

6. Jesus is the perfect revelation of God.

Nobody has ever seen God, who is invisible (1 Tim. 6:16). God became visible by becoming a human. Therefore, to see Jesus is to see God (John 14:9). Jesus has revealed God (John 1:18). He is the visible image, or means of revelation, not merely a reflection (Col. 1:15; 2 Cor. 4:4). He is the perfect full revelation of God in all His nature and attributes (Heb. 1:3). He veiled His glory for most of the time He was on earth, except for the brief moment on the Mount of Transfiguration (Matt. 17:1–2). But He revealed God in other ways by what He did and said. And He continues to do this today, primarily in salvation.

7. Jesus is not a created being.

Contrary to what the Jehovah's Witnesses say, Jesus was not a created being, but the Creator Himself (John 1:2–3, 10; Col. 1:16; 1 Cor. 8:6; Heb. 1:2; Rev. 3:14). Nor was He an angel, which is a created being. Hebrews 1:4–14 explicitly says that Jesus was not an angel. Angels worship Christ. Hebrews 2:7–16 denies that Jesus became an angel to save angels. He was God who became a man to save men. Jesus created the angels (Col. 1:16). The human nature of Christ was created, but not His divine nature.

8. Jesus worked miracles.

While prophets and apostles worked miracles by the power of God and not their own power, Jesus worked miracles by His own divine power. He healed sicknesses, raised people from the dead, cast out demons, stopped storms. The theme of Mark's Gospel is, "Who is Jesus?" He gave them clues in His miracles, until finally some people realized by faith that He was God (Mark 8:27–29). He did what only God could do. They responded like the magicians in Egypt who said, "This is the finger of God." Jesus worked miracles in conjunction with the Father and the Spirit, but not in the way that the apostles did. Jesus frequently claimed to do them by His own power and said that they were "signs" that proved just who He is.

9. There is no salvation for those who deny the deity of Christ.

According to the Bible, we are saved by believing the gospel of who Jesus is and what He did. He died and rose for us. Who is He? God and man. To be saved, one must believe that Jesus Christ is God. Therefore, those who deny His deity are not saved, and they will never become saved until they acknowledge that He is God. John 8:24, "You will die in your sins . . . if you do not believe that I am." The deity of Christ is no secondary doctrine; it is of the very essence of Christianity and salvation.

10. Jesus deserves our worship.

Being God, Jesus deserves our faith. Dying for us, He deserves our love. And He also deserves our worship, which is reserved for God alone. He deserves more than our respect and admiration—He deserves worship. He demands it and His people willingly give it to Him. The angels worship Him (Heb. 1:6). All sinners will bow the knee to Him at the last judgment and confess that He is

Lord (Phil. 2:9–11). People came in faith to Christ on earth and worshiped Him, starting with the wise men (Matt. 2:2, 11). We find example after example of this in the Gospels (e.g., Matt. 8:2; 9:18; 15:25; 28:9; Mark 5:6). They did this in His very presence, and He did not stop them—indeed, He was pleased with it (Matt. 14:33; 28:17). Peter (Acts 10:25–26); Paul (Acts 14:11–18); and angels (Rev. 19:10; 22:8–9) strictly refused such worship. Spurgeon said, "You will never be ready for Heaven unless you are prepared to worship Jesus Christ as God." We begin to worship Him as God now and will worship Him as God forever and ever in Heaven.

28

The Humanity of Christ

1. Jesus became a man.

Jesus Christ was eternally God. At the appointed time, He became a man by being born of a woman (Gal. 4:4). He "came into the world to save sinners" (1 Tim. 1:15). He was not eternally human, nor was He human when He appeared in various manifestations in the Old Testament. He "became flesh" (John 1:14). This is called the *incarnation*. He took on a human body and soul, and became the God-man. He is still the God-man. He became a male, started as a baby, and grew through the stages of life (Luke 2:52).

2. Jesus's deity was not confined to His humanity.

When He became man, He did not cease being God. Deity is omnipresent; humanity is not. There was and is still something "extra" outside of His human nature, namely, His deity. This is sometimes called the *extra Calvinisticum*, because Calvinists believe in it and Lutherans do not. When His human nature was on earth, His divine nature was still everywhere including Heaven (John 3:13, in most translations). His human nature was limited to certain places, such as when the angel said at the empty tomb: "He is not here" (Mark 16:6). The ocean cannot fit into a teacup. He is now with us everywhere in His deity (Matt. 28:20), but His humanity is in Heaven (Heb. 9:24).

3. Jesus was born of a virgin.

Matthew 1 and Luke 1 teach that Jesus had a human mother and a divine Father, but no human father and no divine mother. Mary was a virgin at the time of His conception, even up to the time Jesus was born. Jesus was conceived in her womb by the special miracle of the Holy Spirit (Luke 1:35). This is the only virginal conception and birth in history, a unique miracle. It guaranteed that Jesus would be both God and man and would be sinless.

4. Jesus had two natures in one person.

The Lord Jesus was unique in several ways. He was the only time God became a man, and He was the only man who was also divine. He had two natures. We call this the *hypostatic union*. It is an incomprehensible mystery, worthy of awe and wonder. His deity was not humanized, nor was His humanity deified. The two natures were not mingled or confused, nor was there a third hybrid produced. The two natures are distinct but not separate. He has only one person, not two. He was thus fully God and fully man, not half God and half man.

5. Jesus had a human body.

Jesus became the Second Adam (Rom. 5:14–19; 1 Cor. 15:21–22). He took on a body of flesh and blood. He was not a mere spirit (Luke 24:39). Deity is a pure spirit, incapable of death. Jesus took on a body so that He could die for us. He did not take on an angelic nature to save angels, but a human body and soul to save humans (Heb. 2). "The Word became flesh" (John 1:14). Many of the early Gnostics denied this. They said flesh is necessarily evil and so Jesus was but a ghost. This was rebuked in 1 John 4:2–3 as anti-Christian and demonic heresy. Jesus had a body the same as ours, except for the effects of sin (Phil. 2:8; Heb. 2:14; 4:15). His body was never sick and had no scars until the crucifixion. Yet He grew, had haircuts, ate, drank, slept, grew tired, etc. It was a tangible body that could be seen, touched, and heard (1 John 1:1–2). Of special note is the fact that His body had blood, untainted by sin, with which He made the atonement (1 Peter 1:19).

6. Jesus had a human soul.

Some early heretics say Jesus had a human body and a divine soul and no more. Scripture says He had a human soul in all its various parts and aspects. He had a human mind. Since humanity is limited, His human mind grew in knowledge and was not omniscient (Luke 2:52). He did not know the time of His second coming (Mark 13:32). He also had human emotions. He knew joy and grief. He wept for Lazarus and for others. He had a human will. He submitted it to the divine will: "Not as I will, but as You will" (Matt. 26:39). He had a memory, a conscience, a heart. He was fully human.

7. Jesus was sinless.

Two things differentiated Jesus from us: He was divine, and He was sinless. Since He had no human father, He inherited no original sin (Luke 1:35). Adam and Eve were only temporarily innocent; Christ was permanently sinless. In fact, He was also perfectly sinless. He was impeccable. Though He was tempted in all points as we are, He did not sin (Heb. 4:15). And He could not sin. The union of His deity and humanity was such that all temptations could only fail, for deity cannot sin. He was not only sinless and innocent, but perfectly and uniquely holy, even in His humanity. He was a perfect man. He had a perfectly pure conscience.

8. Jesus veiled His deity.

Though He was still divine, Jesus cloaked His deity under the veil of His humanity. Thus, most people saw just a man. Some saw a good man, others a bad man. Even His relatives thought He was just another man (John 7:5). Philippians 2 describes the stages of Christ's humbling Himself. The first was the incarnation. The second was the humiliation of not being recognized and worshiped as was His rightful due as God. This is the great humility of Jesus. Yet, God the Father and the Holy Spirit knew who He was, as did the angels and even the demons (Mark 1:24).

9. Jesus was our example.

The Lord Jesus served as the perfect example for us in many ways. He did not sin. He did not fight back, lose His temper, slander others (1 Peter 2:21–23). The great passage in Philippians 2 begins by calling on us to imitate Christ's attitude of humility. A famous book developed the theme of how we should always pause and ask ourselves in every situation, "What would Jesus do?" Of course, there were some things in Him that cannot be fully imitated. We cannot die as a propitiation for sin, do miracles by our own power, be worshiped, etc. But those generally refer to His divine attributes. His perfect humanity is the example to follow in all things good and godly, such as love (John 13:34).

10. Jesus had a unique family.

Joseph was his stepfather. Jesus was raised by him and followed him in the family carpentry business (Mark 6:3). Joseph was a "righteous man" (Matt. 1:19 ESV), but not perfect. He was justified by believing in his stepson. Jesus honored Joseph and Mary and kept the fifth commandment (Luke 2:51). Evidently Joseph died before Jesus began His ministry, for we never read of him after Luke 2 except in the past tense. And Jesus, at the cross, committed Mary to the care of John (John 19:26–27). Mary was a virgin in the incarnation and birth, but was not a permanent virgin, as Catholicism teaches. Nor was she sinless; she too needed a Savior (Luke 1:47). She did not ascend into Heaven physically. Jesus had four half-brothers and at least two half-sisters, born to Joseph and Mary (Matt. 13:55–56), who did not believe in Him until after the resurrection (Acts 1:14). Jesus never married or had children. But all true believers are His brethren (Matt. 12:50), His children (Heb. 2:13), and His bride (Eph. 5:25).

29

The Atonement

1. Jesus obeyed the law for us.

Our Lord Jesus was perfectly innocent, pure, and sinless. By obeying the law of God and never sinning, He was thus uniquely able to provide the only sinless sacrifice to His Father. The Old Testament sacrifices could not have any blemishes or faults (Ex. 12:5). Moreover, Christ also obeyed the law in our stead. We call this the *active obedience* of Christ as well as His *vicarious obedience*. Romans 5 says that the disobedience of Adam brought sin and death into the world; the obedience of Christ brought righteousness and life.

2. Jesus was crucified.

He came to die. After thirty-three years waiting and working, including three years of ministry, Christ was betrayed by Judas and was falsely condemned by two unjust trials. God ordained that He die by crucifixion (Acts 2:23). It was a Roman method, not a Jewish one, and extremely cruel and painful. Jesus was "[hung] on a tree" (Deut. 21:22–23; Gal. 3:13), not by ropes but by nails in His hands and feet. It was a public and shameful execution, recorded in all four Gospels. Hung up between Heaven and earth, the Lord Jesus was fastened to the cross like the animals were tied to the altar in the temple (Ps. 118:27), for the cross was His altar. The cross is called a "tree" in 1 Peter 2:24, referring to Deuteronomy 21:23 and the tree motif in the Old Testament (garden of Eden, etc.).

3. Jesus took our sins upon Himself.

It says in 1 Peter 2:24 that Jesus took our sins upon Himself. Isaiah 53:4 says He carried them on Himself like a heavy burden. God laid our sins upon Him, treated Him as if He were the sinner. God "made Him who knew no sin to be sin for us, that we might become the righteousness of God in Him" (2 Cor. 5:21). This was the first part of what is called the *divine exchange*. Our sins were *imputed* to Christ; His righteousness is imputed to us. This does not mean that Jesus was literally made sin or a sinner, but rather was treated "as if" He were sin. The second part of this awesome process was that, being made sin, He then "[became] a curse for us" (Gal. 3:13). God looked at Him as sin, and the thrice-holy God cursed Him and unleashed the floodgates of divine wrath against Him.

4. Jesus suffered for us.

"Christ also suffered for us" (1 Peter 2:21). He suffered the ignominy of not being recognized and worshiped for thirty-three years. This intensified to the very end. He agonized in Gethsemane, even sweating drops of blood (Luke 22:44). He was laughed at, mocked, beaten with sticks, and whipped (Matt. 26:67). The crucifixion itself was excruciating. But the internal pains were even greater. He suffered the very wrath of God in His soul. He drank the cup of wrath and internalized it (Matt. 26:42). By so doing, His sacrifice was the *propitiation* that appeased the Father's wrath (1 John 2:2; 4:10;

Rom. 3:25). It was the only thing that could satisfy all the requirements of the law. God accepted the sacrifice.

5. Jesus shed His blood for us.

The animal sacrifices in the temple were types of Christ in several ways: alive and suffering and shedding blood. But Jesus was no animal—He was a human sacrifice (Heb. 7:27; Eph. 5:2). He shed His blood as a special part of the sacrifice. Without this blood, there could be no atonement or forgiveness (Heb. 9:22). It was sinless, "precious" blood (1 Peter 1:19), infinite in value. One drop alone was worth more than a thousand universes. God gave blood to us to be life in the flesh and for Christ for sacrifice (Lev. 17).

6. Jesus paid the price for our redemption.

Jesus bought us (1 Cor. 6:20). He paid the ransom price to free us from sin and the wrath of God. The price was not paid to Satan, to whom it was not due, but to the Father, whose wrath was over us. Christ "[gave] His life as a ransom" (Mark 10:45). The price was His life and His death. Our sins incurred an infinite debt, not because they are infinite in number or quality, but because they are committed against an infinitely holy God. We owed an infinite debt, which only the infinite God could pay. But man must pay it. So God became man to pay it to Himself. This is the great doctrine rediscovered by Anselm.

7. Jesus died as a substitute.

Jesus had no sins of His own, and therefore did not have to die (Luke 23:41). He would still be alive on earth today had He not done what He did. But He died in our place. This is called the *vicarious atonement*. He stood in our place; He took what we had coming (1 Peter 3:18). And He did this voluntarily. Nobody took His life from

Him. He laid it down of His own accord (John 10:18). He could have called down thousands of angels to stop the crucifixion (Matt. 26:53), but He didn't. "Christ died for us" (Rom. 5:8).

8. Jesus died for all men but especially the elect.

God loves all men, and especially the elect. Just as a husband loves all people but especially His wife, so Christ died for all people but especially His bride. On the one hand, there is a general sense in which Jesus died for all men everywhere (2 Cor. 5:14; 1 Tim. 2:4–6). This is the basis for the free offer of the gospel. But Jesus also died in a special sense for the elect (Eph. 5:25; John 10:15–18; 15:13–14; Isa. 53:8). He died for all, but not equally for all (1 Tim. 4:10). He made salvation possible for all, but He made it definite for His people in particular. He bought some blessings for all men and all blessings for some men.

9. Jesus defeated Satan.

There are many aspects of the atonement. In the Godward direction, it was *propitiation* (Rom. 3:25)—it satisfied God's wrath. In the man-ward direction, it was *expiation*—it took away sins. But there was a third aspect. Satan-ward, it defeated the devil. Jesus came to die, and His death secured the defeat and overthrow of Satan (Heb. 2:14; 1 John 3:8). It also defeated the demons (Col. 2:14–15). Genesis 3:15 predicted when Christ would crush Satan's head by incurring injury to Himself. He slew the great Dragon and freed the fair maiden, the church. He overthrew the Prince of Darkness (John 12:31). He did not negotiate with Satan. He resisted all Satan's temptations and tricks, for Satan had nothing in or on Him (John 14:30).

10. Jesus displayed the love of God.

No man can show greater love to a friend than by dying for him (John 15:13). Christ died for His friends while they were still His enemies (Rom. 5:10). "God demonstrates His own love toward us, in that while we were still sinners, Christ died for us" (Rom. 5:8). Christ showed us just how much He loved us by dying for us (1 John 3:16). This is the greatest display of love imaginable, that God would let His only Son die in the place of enemies (1 John 4:9–10; John 3:16). Surely if God loved us enough to give us the greatest gift of all, Christ, then He will give us everything else (Rom. 8:32). Just as the love of God itself in an unfathomable ocean of undeserved goodness, so the work of Christ is awesome and overwhelming. It alone can finally break these hard hearts of ours and melt them into hearts of loving gratitude.

30

The Resurrection of Christ

1. Jesus was buried.

After He was crucified and died, Jesus was taken down from the cross and buried in a borrowed tomb (Matt. 27:57–61). He was not cremated (the Bible does not condone cremation), nor was He frozen, embalmed, or destroyed. He was buried. This proves, among other things, that He really was dead. If, as some have suggested, Jesus merely fainted on the cross, He would certainly have died when placed alone without medical attention in the tomb. He was put there hastily because the Sabbath was approaching, so there was no time for the women to use the burial spices (Luke 23:54–56). Great importance is placed in 1 Corinthians 15:4 on the burial of Christ, as a sort of bridge between crucifixion and resurrection. Once Jesus's body was in the tomb, a seal was placed on the stone covering it, not to be disturbed upon penalty of death (Matt. 27:66). Armed guards watched it.

2. Jesus descended to the underworld.

Where was Jesus before He arose? His body was in the tomb, but His spirit was in the spirit world. The

Apostles Creed says, "He descended to Hell [Hades]," and 1 Peter 3:19 refers to this. He did not suffer in Hell, as some heretics have suggested. Rather, He went and made a proclamation of His victory over the forces of evil. He proclaimed the defeat and doom of the demons and sinners already in Hell. He did not preach the gospel to them, for there is no second chance after death. Second, He then went to paradise and comforted the spirits of saints there and proclaimed His victory for them. See Luke 23:43. So, Jesus did not disappear or disintegrate into nothingness during that interval.

3. Jesus rose physically from the dead.

Jesus did not stay dead. Being the source of life, it was impossible for Him to stay dead (Acts 2:24). He is the Prince of Life (Acts 3:15). The whole Trinity was involved in raising Jesus: the Father (Heb. 13:20), the Spirit (Rom. 8:11), and Jesus Himself (John 10:18). It was a real physical body, too, not a ghost (Luke 24:39). It was tangible (John 20:27). It still had the scars of the nails and the spear. It was a real resurrection, not a resuscitation, metaphor, or mistake. Throughout the book of Acts, the early Christians boldly proclaimed that Jesus rose from the dead. The resurrection is an essential doctrine of the Christian faith (1 Cor. 15:3–4).

4. The body of Jesus was glorified.

In one sense, the body of Jesus was the same. It was not less than physical. It had the same fingerprints and DNA code. But in another sense, it was different. It was more than physical. It had new properties. For example, it could go through doors (John 20:19), disappear (Luke 24:31), travel great distances in a moment, change appearance (Mark 16:12), etc. Each of the four Gospels records instances of these. It was not only perfect and free from sin, as it had been before, but now was the door to a new kind of human existence. It was the bridge to the next world.

5. God vindicated Jesus.

Romans 1:4 says that God declared Jesus to be the Son of God by the resurrection. God proved that Jesus was who He said He was and vindicated Him. Everything Jesus said and did up to then hung on whether He would rise from the dead. It was a sort of gamble, as it were, so far as others were concerned. If He stayed dead, then He wasn't the Messiah; but if He rose, then He was. He was both victim and victor. God accepted the atonement and showed it by raising Jesus again. Jesus triumphed over death and Satan. If He did not, Christianity is a fraud (1 Cor. 15:15).

6. Jesus appeared to many witnesses.

Each of the Gospels records how Christ appeared to witnesses: the apostles, the women who brought spices (especially Mary Magdalene), the two disciples on the road to Emmaus, and so on. We are not told if He appeared to His mother, Mary, but this is probably true. Judas had already committed suicide (Matt. 27:5), so he witnessed neither the death nor resurrection of Christ. In fact, Christ appeared only to His followers. This strengthened their faith. He did not appear to the Pharisees. He did, though, appear to James His half-brother (1 Cor. 15:7) and probably the rest of His family, and this would have led to their conversion. He appeared to five hundred people at one time (1 Cor. 15:6). Paul was the last one to witness the resurrected Christ (1 Cor. 15:8). Stephen, John, and others had special visions of Jesus in glory, but we have no license to expect such visions today.

7. Jesus was the firstfruits of resurrection.

God had raised others from the dead before Christ

(Lazarus, Jairus's servant, the little girl, a few in the Old Testament), but they later died. The point is that Christ was the first to be raised in a perfect body suitable for Heaven. He is the "firstfruits," or prototype, of our future resurrection, according to 1 Corinthians 15:20. We will be raised in the same kind of body He had (Phil. 3:21). We will live because He lives (John 14:19). Nobody else has received this kind of body yet. It will happen at the rapture (1 Cor. 15:51–54).

8. Jesus returned to Heaven.

After forty days with His people, Jesus returned to Heaven from where He came (Acts 1:10). This is what we call the *ascension*. He ascended from where He had descended thirty-three years earlier (John 3:13; Eph. 4:9–10). This was to complete the Heavenward direction of the resurrection. Acts 1 tells us that the ascension was witnessed by the eleven apostles, and that it was physical and visible and occurred through a cloud. The second coming will be like this in reverse. He was "received up in glory," 1 Tim. 3:16 says. His humanity went up and is not with us, but His deity is everywhere. Thus, He gave the Great Commission of Matthew 28, telling us to go everywhere because He will be with us everywhere, though He is also in Heaven. Enoch and Elijah ascended, but not in this same manner (John 3:13; Heb. 11:5; 2 Kings 2:11). The Catholic Church errs in saying that Mary also ascended without dying.

9. Jesus was crowned Lord of Lords.

Jesus had always been eternally God. But His humanity began at the incarnation and had always lived in humility. Now, the God-man was glorified in His fullness. He was rewarded for His great work of coming down, dying, and rising. Philippians 2 is the great Bible passage on this wonderful theme. He was crowned as

Lord in a special way. For one thing, He now sits on the throne with God the Father. Also, the Father has given all judgment to the Son, the God-man (John 5:22). This is part of the reward and honor bestowed upon Him at the ascension. No doubt the angels in Heaven sang a new song of worship, as did the saints who were there.

10. Jesus now intercedes for us in Heaven.

Between the ascension and second coming, there is the *heavenly session* of Christ. He reigns, answers prayer, and mediates in all things between God and us. He is still the God-man. He did not cease to be God at the incarnation and did not cease to be man at the ascension. He is our Mediator, the only Mediator (1 Tim. 2:4–5). He always lives in Heaven to intercede for us at the bar of God (Heb. 7:25). He prays for us. We daily sin, so we need His daily intercession. He died once but lives forever (Rom. 6:9). We have access to God now through Him (Eph. 2:18). Since there is but one such Mediator, we may not pray through anyone else. And we ought to regularly worship Him and pray to Him.

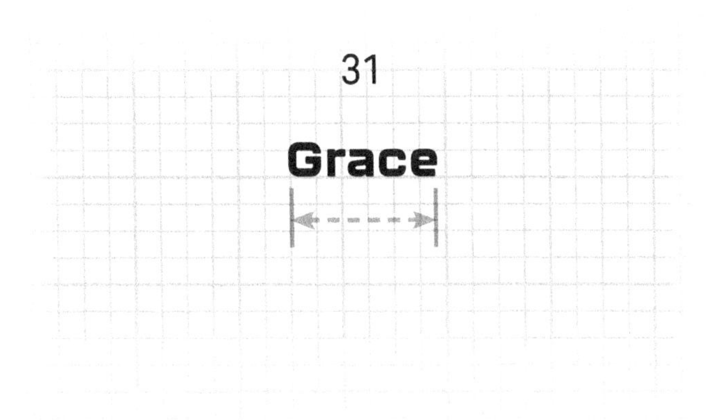

1. No one deserves grace.

Grace is one of the most beautiful words in the Bible. It is that part of God's love that deals with our guilt. In Hebrew, it is *hesed,* sometimes translated as "loving-kindness" or "steadfast love" and refers also to God's covenant love for His people. In Greek, *grace* is translated *charis*. It is free and undeserved. Nobody can merit this grace. Grace is the undeserved love of God for sinners. Unfallen angels know love, but not grace. Fallen sinners can never earn God's grace. By its very definition it is unearned (Rom. 11:6). We earn death by our sin, but grace is a free gift (Rom. 6:23).

2. We are saved by grace alone.

Salvation is completely *sola gratia*, by grace alone. It is not partly by God's grace and partly by our efforts. "By grace you have been saved" (Eph. 2:5, 8). It is solely by God's free, unmerited mercy to us (Titus 3:5). There is no exception; anyone ever saved has been saved by free grace. And the grace comes from God, not from man. Grace being free does not make it cheap or worthless. Quite the opposite. It is beyond cost. We could never earn it in a million years. This is why it is so amazing, matchless, and wonderful. In fact, the original meaning of *charis* was "that which produces joy," something delightful and beautiful.

3. God gives grace to whomever He wills.

Since it is undeserved and free, God is not obliged to give it to anyone. Indeed, He could have justly withheld it from everyone. But He chose to bestow it on some. It is sovereign grace, or sovereignly bestowed on whomever God is pleased to give it to. God said, "I will have mercy on whomever I will have mercy" (Rom. 9:15; see also Ex. 33:19; Rom. 9:18). The word *will* here means "choose." God chose to give His grace and chose the ones to whom He will give it. Is it not His sovereign prerogative to give it to whomever He chooses (Matt. 20:15)? Therefore, God is magnanimous when He gives it to some and cannot be blamed if He decides to withhold it from others. Neither deserved it anyway.

4. God has a special love for some men.

God chose to set this special love on some sinners and not on others. He decided to give His free grace to some, but not all. We have already seen in these studies that God has a general love for all men as His creatures (Matt. 5:44–45; Pss. 33:5; 145:9). That is common grace, the love which God has for all men in common. It is His universal benevolence. But then there is also *special grace*, also known as *particular grace*. It is a greater and different kind of love. It is extraordinary, not ordinary. Just as a man loves all people but especially his wife, so Christ loves all people but especially those He has chosen to be His wife (Eph. 1:4; 5:25). God loves all men with some love, but He loves some men with all love. It is a distinguishing and directed love.

5. God chose some sinners to be saved.

Out of this special grace, God chose some sinners to be rescued from their sins. This is the doctrine of *election.* It happened in eternity past (Eph. 1:4; 2 Thess. 2:13; 2 Tim. 1:9). God sovereignly chose some sinners to be saved from their sins and not to be punished for them (1 Thess. 5:9; 2 Thess. 2:13). They were chosen to receive grace, not wrath. They were chosen individually by name and their names were written in the Book of Life (Rev. 13:8, 17:8, Luke 10:20). God chose us; we did not choose Him (John 15:16). He chose us solely by consulting with His own counsel, not by foreseeing our choice (Eph. 1:11).

6. God made a covenant to save the elect.

Back in eternity, God made a covenant within Himself. The Father chose some sinners to be saved and gave them to the Son, who agreed to die for them (John 17:2, 6, 9, 24). We call this the *covenant of redemption.* We did not even exist at the time, nor was that necessary. It was only necessary that we would exist in time. God sealed this covenant with an oath, thus guaranteeing that we would most definitely be saved at the right time. And in time, God worked out this covenant through Christ, which we call the *covenant of grace.* Special grace was thus given to us in eternity "in Christ" (2 Tim. 1:9). We were chosen in Christ, by Christ, and for Christ. It is definite and sure, not merely possible.

7. God calls the elect in a special way.

Just as God loved all men but especially the elect, so He calls all men to be saved, but especially the elect. God invites all men; we call this the *general call* or the *free offer.* It is what we do in evangelism. But God also gives a *special call,* which is given only to the elect. The parable of Luke 14:16–24 illustrates this. First God invites everyone, then He sends and compels some of them to come in. The general call is given by men; the special call is by God alone. The first is audible, the second is inaudible to the natural ear. It is the Good Shepherd calling His sheep; the others do not hear His voice (John 10:3, 16, 26–27). It is given through the general call, not in some mystical inner voice. "Many are called, but few are chosen" (Matt. 22:14).

8. Saving grace is irresistible.

This special call is by grace. The general call is resistible - indeed, sinners always successfully resist it (Acts 7:51). But the special call cannot be successfully resisted, for God overcomes all resistance. He exerts His omnipotence and overwhelms the sinner's will. He makes us willing in the day of His power (Ps. 110:3). He "compels" us to come in (Luke 14:23). He "draws" us in (John 6:44). Yet it is not raw force, but a holy power and a sweet wooing. He draws us with the irresistible song of grace (Jer. 31:3; Song 1:4; Hos. 11:4). It is heavenly romance, for Christ irresistibly wins the hand of His bride. God thus changes our wills and we come willingly (Ps. 65:4). This is *irresistible grace.*

9. God left the rest of sinners in their sins.

Back in eternity, God sovereignly chose some sinners by His free love. But He did not choose to bestow this grace on all men. He withheld it from some. He owed them nothing but wrath and left them under that wrath. Therefore, nobody can argue that it was not fair. This is the doctrine of *reprobation*. In eternity, God divided the lump of sinful mankind into two parts, like a potter with clay (Rom. 9:21). He left some in their sins. He did not write their names in the Book of Life (Rev. 13:8; 17:8.). He never knew them in special love (Matt. 7:23). He thus predestined them to be punished for their sins (1 Thess. 5:9; Prov. 16:4).

10. God hardens the reprobate's hearts.

God softens the hearts of the elect by His grace, but He hardens the hearts of those He has not chosen. He hides the light of the gospel from them (Matt. 11:25) and blinds them (Rom. 9:18; 11:7; John 12:39–40). He fattens them up for the slaughter they deserve. They do not resist this procedure, but willingly comply, for they love their sins even unto death and Hell. Election and reprobation are two parallel lines running from eternity past to eternity future, ending in Heaven for some and Hell for others. One glorifies God's grace, the other His wrath (Rom. 9:22–23).

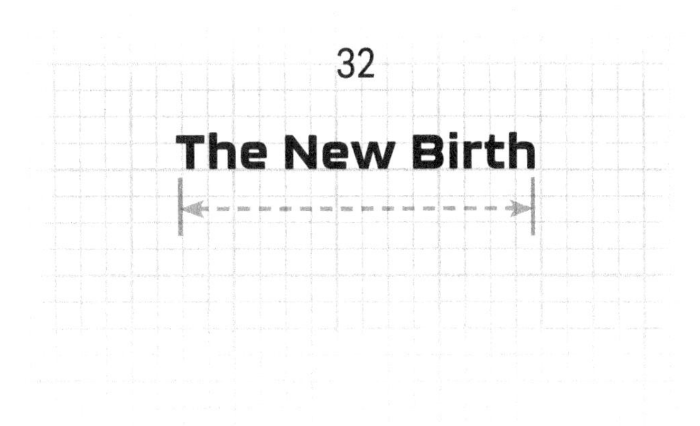

32
The New Birth

1. Man must be born again to enter Heaven.

The Bible uses several terms and analogies to describe salvation. One of them is *regeneration*, or the new birth. John 3 is the classic chapter on the subject. Unless one is born again, he cannot see or enter Heaven. The word can be translated "again" or "from above." Both are true. We must be born a second time from Heaven. We enter this world by physical birth; we are made ready for the next one by spiritual rebirth. We are dead in sins and need this new life to be saved. Those who are not born again do not go to Heaven, but to Hell. Those who are born once will die twice, but those who are born twice will die once (John 11:26; Rev. 20:6).

2. Regeneration is not reincarnation.

The new birth is not a physical one. We do not reenter our mother's womb (John 3:4), nor that of another mother, whether human or animal. Hinduism and Buddhism both teach the error of reincarnation. But this is not to be confused with the Bible doctrine of regeneration. We are born physically once, we die physically once. See Hebrews 9:27. There are no after-death experiences, as sensationally reported. Some of the Jews evidently were influenced by pagan ideas when they thought that Jesus was the reincarnation of John the Baptist, Jeremiah, or other prophets (Matt. 16:14). Also, we will be resurrected in the future in new and better bodies, but not reincarnated in different bodies. Regeneration is a grand truth, while reincarnation is a dangerous heresy.

3. God convicts a sinner before conversion.

Just as a physical birth has birth pains, so does the spiritual birth. It is called conviction of sin (John 16:8). The Holy Spirit does this as He prepares us for the new birth. He takes the holy law of God and burns it into our consciences in a deeper way than ever before. We do more than feel guilty; we know we are lost and doomed. The Puritans used to call this a *law-work* (not to be confused with a work of the law). It is painful and devastating. We resist it, and the more we fight it the worse it becomes. It is painful to kick against God's work (Acts 26:14). God thus breaks open the soil to plant the seed. Conviction is the needle of the law piercing us in order to pull the thread of salvation. No conviction, no conversion. But God turns the pain to joy in due time.

4. The Holy Spirit alone gives the new birth.

John 3 says that we must be born by the Spirit. Our parents gave us natural life, but they cannot give us supernatural life. Our spirits must be regenerated by the Holy Spirit. John 1:13 tells us that this new birth is not produced by parents or even our own wills. God Himself gives the new birth (James 1:18). God never says, "Regenerate yourself." A dead man cannot give himself life. Jesus raised Lazarus. Man is totally passive in regeneration. It is solely the work of the Spirit.

5. Baptism does not produce regeneration.

One of the most damnable and popular heresies is *baptismal regeneration*. It is taught by the Catholic Church, Greek Orthodoxy, Lutheranism, the Church of Christ, the Christian Church, the Disciples of Christ, Episcopalianism, and others. It manufactures false Christians, whether as infants or adults. But water does not produce regeneration. Baptismal water is not magic "holy water." Cornelius was regenerated before baptism (Acts 10:44–48). The dying thief was never baptized (Luke 23:40–43). Simon Magus was baptized but died unregenerate in his sins (Acts 8:13–23).

6. The Word of God is the means of regeneration.

If water is not the means, what is? The Bible. God compares it to a seed (Luke 8:11). We may plant it by telling people the gospel, and another person may water the seed by explaining the Bible to him. But it lies dormant in the sinner's dead heart unless God germinates it (1 Cor. 3:6). God works on the seed by special grace, causing it to break open and produce life in the sinner's heart. The Bible is thus the means of irresistible grace producing the new birth (James 1:18; 1 Peter 1:23). Those who never get this seed will never be saved (Rom. 10:14). Nor does God work this miracle in everyone who hears the gospel. Nor does God produce regeneration without this seed.

7. Regeneration precedes faith.

A dead man cannot move, speak, walk, etc. A dead sinner cannot do anything that requires spiritual life, such as believing. He must first be given life, then he can believe. Lazarus was raised before he could walk out of the tomb (John 11:43–44). God gives the new birth and then the gift of faith. That is the order. He that believes already has eternal life (1 John 5:1). There is no time lag or interval between them. It is merely a matter of which logically precedes and produces the other.

8. Regeneration changes our basic nature.

When we are regenerated, we do not become angels. We remain humans. But our nature as humans changes. Sin still dwells in us (Rom. 7:17), but now so does grace. The point is that we now have spiritual life. We become a "new creation" (2 Cor. 5:17). It is a spiritual resurrection (Eph. 2:1). It is a radical transformation. Sin affected us totally in every part; now grace affects and changes us in every part. Our new nature is basically regenerate, good, Christlike, spiritual. We have remnants of the old, like a swimmer has seaweed clinging to him as he emerges from the sea. It is not a sinner with some good attached, nor equally good and bad, but primarily regenerate with remnants of sin in us till we die.

9. Regeneration is an instantaneous miracle.

It is a miracle of God, not an act of self-reformation by man. God prepares the heart for it by conviction and other things, but regeneration itself occurs in a moment, in the twinkling of an eye. It is not gradual or progressive, but instantaneous and sudden. Nobody is half-regenerate, nor more regenerate than someone else. If one dies before regeneration, he goes to Hell; if after, Heaven. In physical birth, there is a gestation period of nine months following conception. This might be paralleled in the spiritual realm by the process by which God gradually prepares one for regeneration in a moment.

10. Only born-again people are real Christians.

All Christians are born again, and all born-again people are Christians. There are no born-again Muslims. Nor are there any Christians who are not born again. *Born-again Christian* could be a misnomer if it is taken to mean that some Christians are not born again. One becomes a Christian by being born again; there is no other way. "You must be born again" (John 3:7). But, of course, not everyone who says he is a Christian really is a Christian. This is sad and tragic. Most Americans say they are Christians, but it is highly unlikely that more than two percent really are. Saying that you are doesn't make it so. It is not whether we say it, but whether we are in fact. And likewise, not everyone who says he is born again really is regenerate (Catholics and other heretics claim to be). It is vital to discern if we really are.

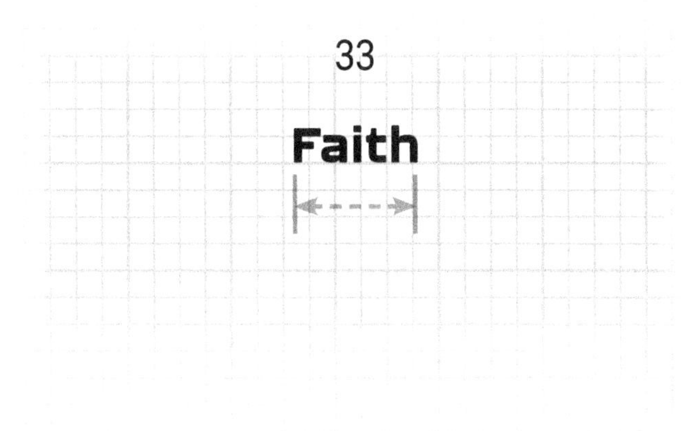

33 Faith

1. Faith is a duty.

All men are required to believe in God as their Creator. They already know He exists; they are called on to agree and submit. Without faith, it is impossible to please God; whoever comes to God must first believe in God (Heb. 11:6). Whatever is not based in faith is sin (Rom. 14:23). This is a general duty imposed on all men as creatures. Those who hear the gospel are further required to believe in Jesus Christ. “Believe in God; believe also in me” (John 14:1). Sinners are commanded, “Believe on the Lord Jesus Christ” (Acts 16:31). It is a duty. In that sense, it is a work (John 6:29). It is something that God commands of us as a duty.

2. We are saved by faith alone.

The Reformers boldly protested Roman Catholicism’s faith-and-works system by proclaiming, “*Sola fide*!” (faith alone). Salvation is by grace alone, through faith alone (Eph. 2:8–9). That is, by grace alone as the source and faith alone as the response. Rome, following the Galatian Judaizers, says that we are saved by faith, but not by faith alone. By faith we receive the sacraments, they say, in order to receive grace that enables us to do enough good works to produce a righteousness in us so as to merit God's approval. This is poisonous heresy. Good works follow faith and salvation, as Ephesians 2:10 shows. The Catholic and Galatian order is this: faith → works → justification. The Bible's order is this: faith → justification → works. We are saved by faith without good works, for the unregenerate sinner is incapable of producing even one good work.

3. There is no merit in faith.

Though faith is a duty, there is no merit in it. We do not earn salvation because of the value of our faith. We do not buy salvation with the coin of faith. Salvation is by grace and cannot be bought by us in any form or fashion, not in whole or in part. To attempt to buy that which is of infinite value is an insult to God. Faith is the instrument of receiving salvation. The value is in the gift, not the hand that receives it. We are not saved on the basis of our faith, but on the basis of the work of Christ. Faith is a duty, but there is no merit in it.

4. Faith agrees with the gospel.

What is faith? Faith has three necessary elements: knowledge, assent, trust. The first means that faith is not blind. It has an object, a content. It is not faith in faith, blind optimism, a positive mental attitude, the power of positive thinking, etc. Second, faith agrees with the true content. The content is the word of God, specifically the gospel. "Believe the gospel" (Mark 1:15). A believer believes that certain things are true. He gives his mental agreement. He is enlightened by the Spirit. He may not understand all the ramifications and implications, but he knows and sees the gospel as true. His heart says, "Amen," which is the Hebrew word for faith (Gen. 15:6).

5. Faith trusts in Christ.

The third and crucial element of faith is trust (Prov. 3:5). The believer trusts Christ personally from the heart (Rom. 10: 9–10). The Bible speaks of believing in, into, and upon Christ, or simply believing Christ Himself. It is not faith in self; it is faith in Christ. It takes Him at His word, trusts in His trustworthiness, and commits to Christ personally.

6. Faith submits to Christ as Lord.

Saving faith also has the element of submission in it, which is part of trust. We are to submit to Christ as a wife is to submit to her husband (Eph. 5:22–24). In conversion, the believing heart accepts Christ's hand in marriage by saying "I do." I do accept and submit. I surrender. I hand Christ the reins, the key, the throne. I bow. They are in serious error who suggest that one may be saved merely by believing in the mind that Jesus is Lord without submitting to Him as Lord in the heart. This part of faith differentiates true believers from false.

7. Repentance is part of faith.

Repentance is a requirement of salvation (Luke 13:3; Acts 3:19). It is not really a second condition but actually part of faith and arises from true faith. Faith has three elements; so does repentance. First, the sinner is convicted of sin and mourns for it as sin (not just because he was caught). He grieves for it (2 Cor. 7:10). Second, he changes his mind about it. He then turns from it (Prov. 28:13). It is more than a change of mind; it is a change of direction from sin to God. Thus, repentance is linked with faith (Mark 1:15; Acts 20:21). It is associated with the word *convert*, meaning "to turn" (Acts 3:19). Unless we turn from sin, we will burn in Hell.

8. Faith is a gift of God.

Faith is a duty, but no man can do that duty. So God gives us the faith that He commands. The Bible often says that faith is a gift (2 Peter 1:1; Phil. 1:29; John 3:27; 6:65; Rom. 12:3; 1 Cor. 4:7). It is given through the Word of God (Rom. 10:17). Faith is not merely offered to us; it is bestowed. It is not held out to be accepted by us if we ask, for James 1:5–7 says that we receive nothing unless we ask in faith. So, God must sovereignly give us that faith. And it is not given to all. Also, repentance is a gift that God gives (2 Tim. 2:25; Acts 5:31; 11:18).

9. Assurance is part of faith.

The Catholic Church denies that anyone can have assurance, but 1 John 5:13 says otherwise. All believers can know that they have eternal life. Moreover, in one sense, all believers have some degree of assurance. They know the gospel is true. They also know that Christ died for them (Gal. 2:20) and that His promise is sure. They have some assurance from the very first moment of faith. But they are not perfected in faith. They still have doubts. So we need to grow in faith and assurance to the "full assurance of faith" (Heb. 10:22). We grow by exercising our faith and feeding on the Word of God, which is the source of faith. The three main tests that confirm faith and evidence assurance are: belief in the true gospel, the evidence of a changed and obedient life (1 John 3:7–10), and the internal testimony of the Holy Spirit (Rom. 8:16). These are the tests that 1 John 5:13 refers to.

10. True faith produces good works.

Faith works by love (Gal. 5:6). "Faith without works is dead" (James 2:26). True faith is a mark of regeneration and will produce works. Life in the root will produce fruit on the branch (Matt. 7:17). Those who do not have good fruit will have only bad fruit, and thereby show that they are still unregenerate. A Christian still sins, but he will not stay in permanent sin. He will keep bearing the fruit of good works. Our new nature cannot be killed and will keep believing and obeying (1 John 3). So, we are not saved by faith and works, but saved by grace through faith so that we may show our gratitude by good works (Eph. 2:8–10).

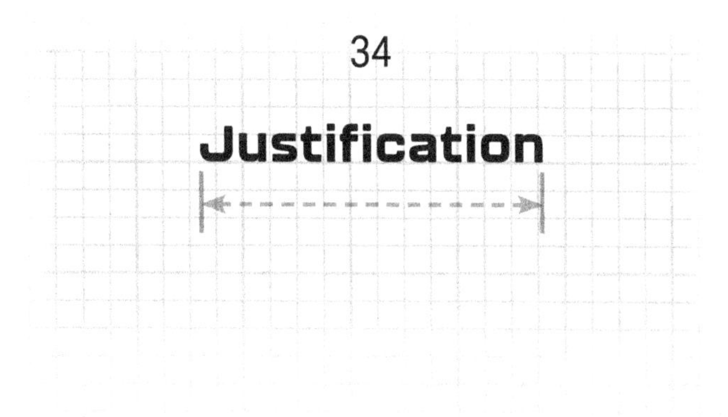

34 Justification

1. Justification is a legal act of God.

One of the most precious aspects of salvation in Scripture is *justification*. It is God that justifies (Rom. 8:33). Self-righteous sinners justify themselves but remain condemned by God (Luke 10:29). God justifies the ungodly (Rom. 4:5), but not by excusing their sin or denying they are sinners. Justification is a legal act by God, a metaphor taken from the law court. The best and most popular definition is in the Westminster Shorter Catechism: "Justification is an act of God's free grace, wherein he pardons all our sins, and accepts us as righteous in His sight, only for the righteousness of Christ imputed to us, and received by faith alone" (Q. 33).

2. Justification is by grace alone.

Salvation is by grace alone and so justification is by grace alone. Romans 3:24: "justified freely by His grace." It is not purchased by us in whole or in part by our good works. We cannot earn it, nor would we if we could. To try to buy it is to offer the Judge a bribe, but God takes no bribes (Ex. 23:8). It is a legal act, but also one of pure grace.

3. Justification is by faith alone.

The Catholic Church, like the early Judaizers, says that justification is by faith and works, not by faith alone. They are not merely saying that works must follow faith; they are saying that both must precede justification. We utterly deny it. Again, they say the order is: faith → works → justification. The Bible says: faith → justification → works. Romans 3:28 and Galatians 2:16 are very explicit that we are justified by faith alone. Faith is the condition. It is not the ground of justification. It is the condition in the sense that God will not justify without it, and it is by faith that we are connected with Christ. He is the true merit.

4. God justifies a person because of the work of Christ.

We are "justified by His blood" (Rom. 5:9). God set forth Christ as the propitiatory sacrifice that appeased His wrath (Rom. 3:25). God thereby looks at the cross, is satisfied, and is then able to justify us. God did not sweep sin under the carpet. He punished it in Christ. The work of Christ, then, is the ground upon which God can legally justify us. We are also justified in His resurrection (Rom. 4:25).

5. Justification is the second part of the great exchange.

One of the Bible's golden verses of salvation is 2 Corinthians 5:21. It speaks of a "great exchange." The first stage took place two thousand years ago. God placed our sins upon Christ. He made Him to be sin. This was not literal. It was by substitution. Christ was treated as if He were the sinner. He was then made a curse (Gal. 3:13). He suffered the wrath of God and died. The second stage is when a sinner believes in Christ. Christ places His righteousness on the sinner, who is then accounted righteous by God. He is treated as if he had never sinned. It is the perfect counterpart of the cross.

He suffered; we can rejoice. He died; we live. We are not literally made righteous in justification, just as He was not literally made sin in the atonement. Our sins were imputed to Him; His righteousness is imputed to us. This is why faith is the proper instrument that connects us with the cross, for we believe that Christ died for us.

6. God imputes the righteousness of Christ to us.

Justify is the legal metaphor; *impute* is the financial metaphor. God put our sins on the account of Christ. Now God puts the righteousness of Christ on our account. He marks the bill "paid in full." He transfers the value of Christ's person and work to our account. Incidentally, God imputes both the active (life) and passive (death) work of Christ to us. See Romans 5:17–19. God then treats us as if we had never sinned. Indeed, He can look at us as clothed in the very righteousness of Christ (Zech. 3:4; Rom. 3:22).

7. God pardons all our sins.

There are two aspects of justification. In the one, God takes away sin. He forgives it (Ps. 103:3). He pardons us (Isa. 55:7). Second, He puts the righteousness of Christ in its place. This completes the great exchange. God pardons all our sins—past, present, and future (Ps. 103:3). God takes away the penalty of guilt. Though we are guilty, He does not hold our sins against us. We are blessed because God no longer imputes sin or its guilt to us (Rom. 4:6–8). God pardons us. He does not grant clemency, which would somehow mitigate our sins. Nor does He place us on probation or parole. He totally pardons every sin we have ever committed (Mic. 7:19). Moreover, He pardons the very sin nature in which we were born.

8. Justification is instantaneous.

God the Judge bangs the heavenly gavel down in a

moment. He does not say, "Not guilty," per se, but rather "Justified!" We are freed in the twinkling of an eye. God predestined in eternity that we would be justified, but we were not actually justified until the moment of faith. Justification is instantaneous and complete. It is not progressive. No one is more justified than another. In fact, those in Heaven are not more justified than the saints on earth, for justification is a perfect legal declaration by God Himself. An auctioneer bangs the hammer "Sold" in an auction to signal the moment the sale is enacted. So too, God bangs the gavel in the court of Heaven. If it did not occur in a moment, what would be the fate of those who died halfway through the process? It must be in a moment. One second before, the sinner is condemned and doomed; one second after, justified forever.

9. Justification is not regeneration.

These two are essential to salvation and are inseparably related but must be distinguished. In regeneration, our nature is changed; in justification, our status is changed. In the former, righteousness is infused; in the latter, it is imputed. The order is: regeneration → faith → justification. But we are not justified on the basis of what God does in us by the new birth. No, the basis is the work of Christ. The new birth is drastic, but in some respects is only partial—we still have indwelling sin. We are not justified by an internal righteousness, but by an alien righteousness (Phil. 3:9). What Christ has done in us is partial and progressive (Phil. 1:6), and so would not provide a complete basis anyway. Also, there is no interval between the two. Some err in suggesting that an infant might be regenerated but not justified till later in life. If so, what if he died at age sixteen: if regenerate, then fit for Heaven; but if unjustified and unbelieving, fit for Hell. It wouldn't make sense.

10. Justification is permanent and irrevocable.

There is no double jeopardy (Rom. 8:33–34). Satan cannot appeal the verdict, raise an objection, or sue for a mistrial. It is over and done with. All that follows is the joy of knowing one is justified and free forever, never to be condemned. We have peace with God at last! (Rom. 5:1).

35

The Benefits of Salvation

1. Christians are saved.

Salvation is the general term that the Bible uses to describe the miracle of grace God performs for us. It is the greatest event in our life. It has three main stages: past, present and future (see 2 Cor. 1:10). We were saved at a point in the past. This is when we were born again, believed, repented of sin, and were justified. It happens only once (born again, not born again and again and again). It is perfect and complete. We were rescued from danger, delivered from harm. Now we are saved and safe. Second, we are being saved in the present. Christ's blood keeps us safe from the wrath of God and He daily rescues us from Satan. Third, we will be saved in the future—at death and at the judgment day. These three stages are inseparable.

2. The Holy Spirit indwells us.

The Spirit enters the believer at the moment of regeneration and never leaves. He enters our whole being, even our body (Rom. 8:9–11). It is the heavenly counterpart to being demon-possessed. He fills us (Eph. 5:18). Romans 8 is the great chapter on the indwelling of the Spirit. Also, this is the miracle of the baptism of the Spirit, misunderstood by Pentecostals. The Spirit comes into us, with the result that He is in us. At the same moment, He puts us into Himself, with the result that we are in the Spirit. He in us, we in Him. It is not a second experience, but part of salvation. From there, we are to walk in the Spirit (Gal. 5:16), go on being filled with the Spirit (Eph. 5:18), etc.

3. The Christian knows God.

Every person knows that God exists (Rom. 1:19), but only the Christian knows God personally. This is real knowledge. It is a heart-to-heart personal relationship. It is part of having eternal life (John 17:3). God granted us this privilege (Matt. 11:27). We know Him because He first knew us (1 Cor. 8:3; Gal. 4:9). It is a personal, deep, and intimate knowledge. We are friends (John 15:14–15). We are also lovers (1 John 4:19; Song 2:16). And we grow in this knowledge deeper and deeper (Phil. 3:8, 10).

4. We are united to Christ.

This is similar to the union of the Holy Spirit. We are put into Christ's Body (1 Cor. 12:13), with the result that we are "in Christ." At the same moment, Christ is put into us and is in us. In one sense, we were united with Him in the eternal covenant, but we were united with Him in our experience when we were saved. We are united to Him and draw life from Him and cannot do anything without Him (John 15:5). We are also united with Him in spiritual espousals. We are engaged to be His bride. One day, this will be consummated at the great heavenly marriage (Rev. 19:7; 21:2).

5. We are adopted into God's family.

Once we were children of the devil (John 8:44). God took us out of that family and made us His own children

(Gal. 4:5). Now God is our Father, other believers are our brothers and sisters, and Christ is our elder brother. Being His children, we are also His heirs (Rom. 8:15–17). We can now call God "our Father in Heaven" (Matt. 6:9). Adoption is not the same as regeneration. Regeneration affects our nature; adoption, our relationship and standing. Regeneration precedes faith, which precedes adoption. But it happens in a moment, with no interval or exception. So, we are doubly God's children.

6. We are reconciled to God.

Reconciliation is a wonderful benefit of salvation that we often overlook. The great passage on it is 2 Corinthians 5. We were once God's enemies; now we are His friends (Rom. 5:10). We are reconciled. It is more than a truce; it is the end of hostilities. The war is over. We have peace with God (Rom. 5:1). We were once against God and God against us. Now He is for us and with us, and we with Him. Properly speaking, it is we that are reconciled to God, not God to us. We apologize, not He. Yet, on His part, the righteous enmity was removed when His wrath was appeased when Christ died for us.

7. We are no longer under wrath.

We were once sinners under the wrath of God—condemned, doomed, facing judgment. All that has changed. We will never be judged. God is not angry with us but smiles on us in fatherly love. God saved us from several things: sin, Satan, death, Hell. But most importantly, He saved us from His own wrath (Rom. 5:9). God saved us from God. Lost sinners are still under His wrath (John 3:36). But not us. As fierce as His wrath was against us then, so intense is His love for us now.

8. We are cleansed from sin.

Our sins were filthy and disgusting. Even our religious acts were filthy rags (Isa. 64:6). But God changed all that. He cleansed us (1 Cor. 6:11). He washed away the black guilt by the blood of Christ (Rev. 1:5). We were baptized in the blood of the Lamb. Our sins were drowned in the Red Sea of His blood. Only Christ's blood, not the waters of baptism, can cleanse us in this way, for water cannot touch the soul. In one sense, we are already totally cleansed (Isa. 1:18). In another, we need daily cleansing for the regular sins we commit (see John 13:10). This does not mean we get saved all over again. It only means that we need fresh applications of the blood of Christ (1 John l:7).

9. We are transferred from Satan's kingdom.

Colossians 1:13 says that God transferred us from the kingdom of darkness into the kingdom of light. Christ, not Satan, is now our King. We defected from Satan's evil empire, became traitors to his wicked regime, and now are spies engaged in espionage and commandos involved in sabotage. We have been rescued from Satan's claws; he can never have us again. We are on another team, part of another body, have different allegiances. We were once for Satan and against God. Now we are against Satan and for God (Matt. 6:24). If God is for us, who can be against us (Rom. 8:31)?

10. We cannot lose our salvation.

One of the great glories of salvation is that it is permanent. It has a ratchet-effect. Once saved, always saved. It is not because of our own selves, or even our own faith. It is ultimately dependent on God, for it was He that saved us in the first place. If it depended on us, none of us would get saved or stay saved. God elected us to salvation (Rom. 8:29–30) and completes what He started (Phil. 1:6). He has sworn to preserve, keep, and guard us forever (Pss. 37:28; 66:9; 97:10; 145:14; 2 Tim. 1:12). He keeps us by His omnipotent hand (1 Peter 1:5); keeps us safe from Satan (1 John 5:18; John 17:11, 12, 15); and seals us with the Holy Spirit (Eph. 1:13; 4:30). The saints in Heaven are happier, but not more secure, than we are. Simply put, God loves His people too much to let them go. He holds us firmly and lovingly in His arms of love, from which no one can snatch us out (John 10:28).

36

Spiritual Growth

1. The new birth is the start of the Christian life.

Regeneration is the end of the old life, but also the beginning of the new life. It is the door out of one and the door into the other. We are like "newborn babes," 1 Peter 2:2 tells us, who need to be fed and grow. A baby needs feeding, teaching, cleaning, exercise, love, etc. No one can live the Christian life until he first gets born again. Then he begins the wonderful lifelong adventure of following and serving Jesus Christ.

2. The Bible feeds and strengthens us.

A baby needs food—milk. The Bible is that milk. It is the food and nourishment and refreshment that we need to grow as Christians. The more we eat, the more we grow (and the less we eat, the less we grow). It is the means of grace—the way in which God continues to supply us with grace. It is compared to milk, bread, meat, and honey. It is sometimes hard to digest, other times very sweet. Feeding on the Word takes the same stages as physical eating. We bite into it by reading it. We chew it by studying it. We swallow it by believing it. We digest it by understanding it. We incorporate it by obeying it.

3. We follow Christ by faith.

We were saved by faith; we continue to follow by faith

(Col. 2:6–7). We continue in the way we started. We walk by faith, not by sight (2 Cor. 5:7). We believe the promises of God, not trust our own feelings. It is as simple as, "Trust and obey, for there's no other way, to be happy in Jesus, than to trust and obey." We follow as His disciples, which means students, learners, pupils. We ought to sit at His feet and learn from Him. That takes faith. It does not happen overnight. It is a school of discipleship from which no one ever graduates until death. Faith is the primary means by which we follow, so we need to exercise our faith, strengthen it, pray for more.

4. We are saved to serve.

We were once slaves of sin and Satan; now we are slaves of righteousness (Rom. 6:16–22). We are slaves of Christ. Not slaves who wish to be free, but willing slaves. We serve Christ as our Master. He purchased us, and we belong to Him and not to ourselves (1 Cor. 6:19–20). Therefore, we ought to serve Him and not ourselves. He wants us to serve Him by serving other people, too. All this involves sacrifice—putting Christ first, others second, ourselves last. It is also a duty. A slave has the duty to serve his master. We have the duty of serving our Lord Jesus Christ. It is not always easy, but it is always right.

5. We serve Christ out of gratitude.

God wants us to obey Him. The Christian is like the Israelites after God delivered them from Egypt. They were grateful and wanted to express it. It was as if God said, "If you want to show how grateful you are, then here's how. Don't have any other gods, don't take my name in vain, etc." We ought to be grateful for all the great blessings which God has given to us for free. With this in mind, the Christian life should be one of joyful gratitude, not dour drudgery. This gives vitality to duty. It is a privilege to serve the Lord Jesus Christ. We sometimes forget and thus become ungrateful. That's why God told us to celebrate the Lord's Supper regularly, to remember His great love at the cross, lest we forget and be ungrateful. When we remember, our faith is renewed, and our gratitude increased.

6. God equips each of us with a spiritual gift.

The members of the body build each other up (Eph. 4:16). This is done by the spiritual gifts which God gives to all Christians (1 Cor. 12; Rom. 12). These are not natural talents, which all have, though God uses those also. Spiritual gifts are the special abilities God gives us to serve Him and other Christians. They are tools, not toys. We need to discover what our own gift is by checking the lists and examples in the Bible, discerning if we have one of them, study how to use it properly—and then use it!

7. We fight against Satan.

The warfare with God is over when we are reconciled to Him, but this begins the warfare with Satan. Better to have God with us against Satan than Satan with us against God (Rom. 8:31). The Christian life is not one of ease and fun, but of struggle against temptation and fighting with Satan. Ephesians 6 is the classic chapter on spiritual warfare. God supplies the armor to defend against Satan's attacks. We are not alone in this fight; every Christian is in the war. And God fights for us, too (Ex. 14:14).

8. Christians face trials.

Christians struggle against temptation as well as against trials and tribulations (James 1:2). We suffer persecution from friends and family. We suffer afflictions of all sorts. This comes with being a Christian and only makes us stronger. It is a sure sign that we are on the right side. It purifies us and tests our faith. There is also a great blessing in the midst of persecution, if we stand for Christ against all odds. Though we sometimes fail the tests and trials, God does not forsake us. We are down, but not out (2 Cor. 4:8–11). God picks us up and keeps us going. The Christian's life is not a bed of roses, but of thorns and tears. But it is worth it all. There is an exquisite joy of being in the fire for Christ.

9. The Christian life is a lifelong walk.

The Bible frequently compares the Christian life with a walk (Eph. 2:10; 4:1, 17; 5:2, 8, 15). It is not a stroll, but a march. It is a hike, the long walk of a pilgrim (we are pilgrims with a destination, not hobos without a home). It is a step-by-step walk, a daily life of obedience. We may stumble in this walk, but we get right back up and keep going. We are to run this race set before us (Heb. 12:1). It is a long-distance marathon, not a short sprint. One of the great Christian books on this theme is *The Pilgrim's Progress* by John Bunyan. It begins in the City of Destruction and ends in Heaven.

10. We look back at the cross and forward to the crown.

It is good to look back and remember our former life, but not yearn for it. It is also important to look back in faith to the cross. This reminds us of why we are on this road to begin with, for sometimes we forget. And it is also important to look forward to the end of the trail. Backward in faith, forward in hope. Our walk is not in vain. It has a goal, a destination. That is Heaven, where we will receive the crown (2 Tim. 4:8). There are rewards for obedience, which serves as added incentive to obey and serve all the more (1 Cor. 3:14; Matt. 25:14–30). When we arrive at the end of the road, we will be met by our blessed Savior. In the meantime, Jesus walks with us every step of the way, strengthening and encouraging us and keeping us on the straight and narrow path.

37

Spiritual Experience

1. God desires us to have true spiritual experience.

God has done many things for us and granted us the privilege of being a Christian. He has blessed us with all spiritual blessings in Heaven (Eph. 1:3). We are positionally right with God. But He also desires us to be what we are. He wants us to be and live in practice what we are in Heaven. We are to be daily transformed into the image of Christ (2 Cor. 3:18). In fact, not just in theory. He has already changed our nature. Now we are to go on being changed gradually. This involves our experience: what we are and what we do. The order is as follows: we believe in our minds, trust in our hearts, speak it with our mouths, and do it with our hands.

2. God develops the fruit of the Spirit in us.

God has changed the root, now He grows fruit on the branches. This is done by the life-giving power of the Holy Spirit who dwells in us. He produces these new attitudes within us. They are listed in Galatians 5:22. They begin internally, then manifest themselves externally. We cannot produce them ourselves. We are connected to Christ the Vine, who produces them in and through us (John 15:1–8). God actually changes the way we think, feel, and look at things. This in turn produces spiritual virtues, such as those listed in Matthew 5:3–9 and 2 Peter 1:5–7.

3. Love is the most important spiritual fruit.

Love is the first fruit listed in Galatians 5:22. It is the greatest of all God's commandments: love God, love other people (Matt. 22:37–40). We are to love others as Christ loved us, even willing to die for them (1 John 3:16). We are told to walk in love (Eph. 5:2). How important is this attitude of love? Without it, all else is worthless (1 Cor. 13). Faith is the primary virtue, but love is the culminating and crowning virtue. Love seeks the well-being of another, seeks to do good to him. God wants us to love in reality. He wants us to really love, not just say it (1 John 3:18), and show it in our deeds. But it begins in the heart, and that means true Christian experience.

4. We sin and backslide.

Though we have been born again, sin still dwells in us (Rom. 7:17). We still sin. We do what we should not do and fail to do what we should do. We develop bad habits of frequent sins. When we sin for a period of time, we call this backsliding (Hosea 14:4). It is like riding a bicycle up a hill: if we stop going forward, we go backward. This sometimes happens with besetting sins, which are like weights that pull us down (Heb. 12:1). We need to be aware and beware of them. Backsliding affects our hearts and we should never get accustomed to sin. We must immediately forsake it.

5. God chastens His children.

Because we are His children, God chastens us (Heb. 12:5–11). He does this out of love, not wrath. It is for our good, not for our punishment. He does it as a Father, not as a judge. God does not chasten us to "get even," but to teach us not to sin. How does God chasten? He does it in a variety of ways: affliction, circumstances, illness, financial loss, etc. He even uses our enemies. Chastening teaches us that sin is not worth it. It always hurts—it's supposed to. But it is for our good and is evidence that we are God's children. Not all the afflictions we suffer are due to sin, but some are. When we are afflicted in some way, we need to pray and search our hearts and Bibles to see if it is because of any specific sin (Ps. 139:23). Chances are that our own consciences will convict us.

6. We must deny ourselves.

Self-denial is another important virtue affecting our experience (Mark 8:34). It is not easy and is never fully mastered in this life. Sin wants us to put ourselves first and this has been the history of our lives. That attitude produces pride. God tells us to deny ourselves, not put ourselves first. He does not want us to engage in self-love, self-esteem, or self-worth, all of which are simply other words for pride. God wants us to be humble (1 Peter 5:5–6). We need to deny our selfishness, our sinful lusts, our desire to be "Number One." Our self must be crucified.

7. We must mortify indwelling sin.

Our basic nature was changed in regeneration, but original sin still dwells in us as an unwelcome stranger. We cannot expel it once and for all. There is no instant perfection, as some teach (1 John 1:8). We daily struggle against it and sometimes give in. We are told to mortify it (Rom. 6). How? Several ways. For one, we are to make no provision for the flesh (Rom. 13:4). Starve it by not giving in to it or providing opportunity for it. Also, we are to reckon sin as a foreign intruder. Then we are to reckon ourselves as alive to Christ and dead to sin (Rom. 6:11). This means, among other things, to believe that we really have changed and that we do not have to sin. We may still struggle and give in, but we also can fight and win those struggles and gain victories and progress. This is an important part of true spiritual experience, but often overlooked.

8. We ought to be separate from the world.

We are in the world but are not to be of the world (1 John 2:15–16). We are to go in and evangelize it, but not let it in and bring us down. The world ought to be able to see a noticeable difference in us. We need different attitudes, words, lifestyles, deeds, even attire. We ought not to indulge in worldly fashions, entertainment, or the like. There ought to be a noticeable difference between us and the world, otherwise we are but hypocrites. We need to be careful lest the world's sin seeps into us and affects the way we think and live. It takes vigilance.

9. We need to examine ourselves.

We are told in 2 Corinthians 13:5 to examine ourselves. The first thing to check is whether we are true Christians or only deceived. We examine our lives by submitting them to God to examine. We look in the mirror of God's Word (James 1:23–25), which will show the imperfections of our character. Indwelling sin likes to deceive us, so it cannot be trusted. We can only trust the Bible to give us a true examination. We need to search and discover our faults, weaknesses, secret sins, bad habits. Then we inspect our overall character and, finally, our words and deeds. One way is to compare ourselves with Christ—we will soon spot the imperfections in us. Also, we need to check and see how much we have progressed so far in the Christian life— how much we have done versus how much we could have done.

10. We have the privilege of enjoying God.

One more thing needs to be pointed out as we conclude this section on spiritual experience. God desires for us to find our joy in Him. We are to love Him and enjoy Him (Ps. 37:4). Love and be loved by God. This produces spiritual delight and true pleasure. We taste and see that the Lord is good (Ps. 34:8). We do this by prayer and Bible study, worship at church, fellowship with the brethren, Communion, and walking closely with the Lord Jesus day by day. With Christ in us and with us, it is then possible to enjoy God's presence even in the little things. This is one of the most delightful aspects of the Christian's experience, a little bit of Heaven on earth.

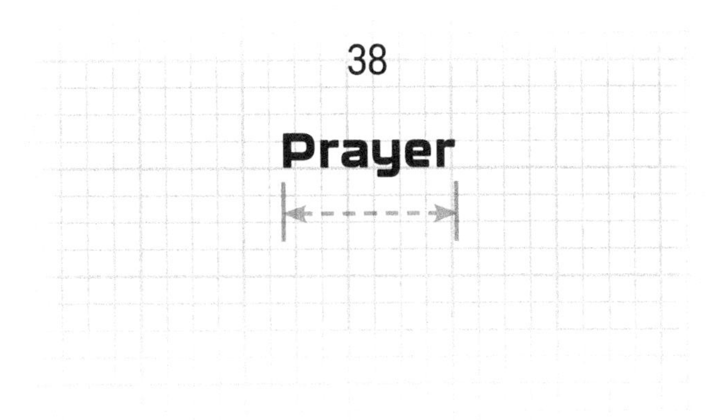

1. Prayer is a great privilege.

One of the most important parts of the Christian life is prayer. It is also one of the most neglected. Yet what a great privilege it is. Imagine being granted the privilege of speaking with God Almighty Himself! Though God rules the whole universe and knows everything, He condescends to listen to us unworthy sinners. It is a privilege, not a right. God lets us approach Him in prayer (Ezek. 36:37). Done rightly, prayer is for our good and for the glory of God.

2. Prayer is a great duty.

Not only is prayer a privilege, it is a duty. All men are duty-bound to ask their Creator for the things they need. In this sense, even unbelievers ought to pray and acknowledge God. Yet God will not hear their prayers until they are converted (John 9:31). As for believers, we are frequently commanded to pray and are given many examples in the Bible. Though God is sovereign, we have the responsibility to pray. In a deep mysterious way, God uses our prayers to carry out His eternal will.

3. We must confess our sins regularly.

There are several aspects of prayer. One of the most important is *confession*. We ought not barge into God's presence with unclean hands. Like the Old Testament priests who were to wash their hands before entering the temple (Ex. 30:20), so we must confess our sins before proceeding further. To confess means to acknowledge and admit, without any excuses (Ps. 51:3). It also means to repent and be willing to turn from sin (Prov. 28:13). We cannot shift the blame onto others, not even Satan, Adam, or other people, least of all God. We have nobody to blame but ourselves and confession means taking the blame. It means submitting to chastening. If we confess our sins, God will forgive them (1 John 1:9). God will cleanse us and restore us to the fellowship with Him that was broken by our sin. Unless we confess our sins, God will not hear our prayers (Ps. 66:18; 1 Peter 3:7).

4. We may ask God for the things we need.

God has granted us the privilege of asking for the things we need. This is called *supplication*. We request these things from God; we cannot demand them by right. See Philippians 4:6. There are many things we do not have because we have not asked for them or because we have asked in the wrong way (James 4:2–3). No request is too small or too large to bring to God. This does not mean that we sit back and do nothing. No, we are to do what we can and open the channels by which God may answer our prayers. For example, we are to ask for our daily bread (Matt. 6:11), but that does not mean we quit our jobs. It is important to keep priorities in their right place when we pray. Spiritual needs are more important than material needs. We ought to pray for food, clothing, work, health, and so on. But we ought to pray even more for growth in grace, humility, more faith, an increase in love, opportunities to witness, and so on.

5. We may ask God for the needs of others.

Asking God for the needs of others is called *intercession* (1 Tim. 2:1). As with supplication, we may ask for the needs of others, especially their spiritual needs. Look at what Paul prayed for in his epistles—1 Timothy 2:1–2 is a good example. We can pray for anyone, especially those in authority, for God's will to be done, for their salvation, etc. It is best to pray mostly for those known to us more than for others less known to us. Information about their needs helps.

6. We must have faith when we pray.

James 1:6 tells us that we must have faith when we pray, otherwise we will not receive what we ask for. This does not mean that we must have giant faith—Jesus said that faith as small as a mustard seed can move mountains by prayer (Matt. 17:20). This does not mean that we can "Name it and claim it," as some teach (Mark 10:35–38). That would be presumptuous. On the other hand, God does not honor lazy prayer. We are to persevere in prayer over and over again (Luke 18:1–3; Eph. 6:18; 1 Thess. 5:17).

7. We must pray to God alone.

God forbids us from praying to anyone else. This is because prayer is a form of worship and we are to worship God alone (Matt. 4:10). We must never pray to any other god, such as Allah. Nor may we pray to angels or Christians in Heaven, as Roman Catholicism teaches. It is one thing to ask another living person to pray for you; it is quite another to ask a dead person to pray for you or answer your prayers. God strictly forbids us from trying to contact the dead (Deut. 18:10–11). Prayer means speaking with God alone. It includes meditation on His Word (Ps. 1:2). This is not transcendental meditation or talking to yourself. God speaks to us in the Bible. We reply in prayer.

8. We can pray anytime anywhere.

We need not be in a church meeting to pray. We may and should pray at any time, such as in an emergency in the middle of the night (Neh. 2:4). We can pray anywhere, too, such as in our cars or in the hospital. For example, it is a good practice to pray before meals, as they did in the Bible (Acts 27:35). We may pray when we are alone or with others. In fact, the Bible gives us examples of group prayer meetings (Acts 12:5, 12; 16:13). This is very important to the health of a church. No church is stronger than its prayer meeting. Also, parents should have daily family devotions with their children to lead them in prayer and Bible reading.

9. Prayer must be in Christ's name.

We must pray based on the merits of Christ, not our own. We do not use the words "in Christ's name" as magic words, but with the meaning that we are relying solely on Christ's worth and authority. We are to pray according to God's will (1 John 5:14–15). We ought not to pray for things God has forbidden or which are outside the scope of prayer. For example, we ought not to pray for certain spiritual blessings for unbelievers which really belong only to believers (see John 17:9). We must pray for the conversion of unbelievers first, then the rest. Prayer must be regulated by God's Word. We must not borrow ideas of prayer from pagan religions, such as burning candles, spinning wheels, using beads, reciting incantations, saying repetitious words, etc. We ought to follow the example of Christ.

10. Worship is the highest form of prayer.

If confession is the low notes on the prayer scale, then worship is the high notes. This is the most important aspect of all, for it alone will continue into eternity. We ought to thank God in prayer. Unthankfulness is a great sin (Rom. 1:21). We ought to praise God, both for what He has done and for what He is in Himself. We should meditate on His word and let our hearts dwell on His person. Worship means to humble ourselves before God and exalt Him as God. It may be vocal, or it may be silent. *Adoration* is the very zenith of this aspect of prayer. Adoration is that beautiful combination of love and worship. It is loving worship and worshipful love. In this God is most glorified, and in it we fulfill the purpose for which we were created. We can find no happier or holier place than the place of true worship.

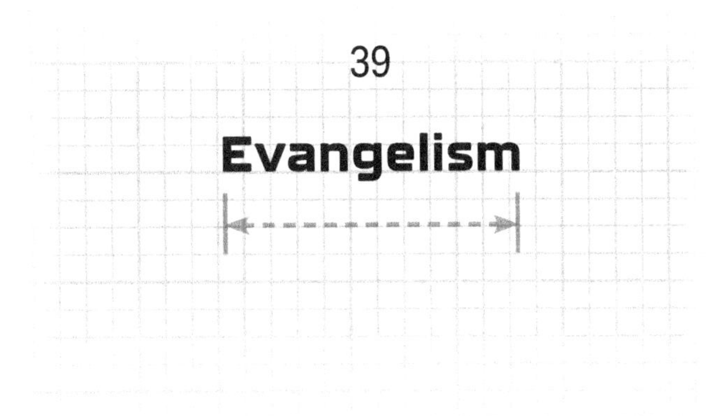

39
Evangelism

1. Christ commanded us to preach the gospel.

Right before He returned to Heaven, Jesus told the apostles to preach the gospel throughout the world. We call this the *Great Commission*. We find it in Matthew 28:18–20; Mark 16:15–16; Luke 24:47; and Acts 1:8. Jesus preached the gospel while He was here (Mark 1:14–15). He is still with us spiritually and through us continues to spread the gospel. The first Christians started in Jerusalem and throughout history Christians have preached the gospel to almost every part of the world. But the work is not yet over. The Great Commission is still a great work.

2. All Christians should spread the gospel.

Obviously, Jesus knew that the first twelve apostles could never cover the whole world, let alone live until the second coming to tell the gospel to people everywhere in all later generations. The work has been passed on to each generation and to each Christian. It is not just for preachers and evangelists—it is for all Christians. Some early Christians were slow to do this, but God providentially stirred them up and sent them out everywhere (Acts 8:4). What an immense impact we would have on the world if every Christian today would do their share in spreading the gospel. Most people who come to Christ do so through the personal evangelism of a friend or relative.

3. Some Christians have the gift of evangelism.

While all Christians are to evangelize, some have the gift to be able to do it better and more often than others. *Evangelists* are mentioned in Ephesians 4:11 and 2 Timothy 4:5. Philip was an evangelist (Acts 21:8). There have been many great evangelists over the centuries, such as George Whitefield and John Wesley. But most with this gift aren't pastors; they are everyday Christians who have the burning desire to tell people the gospel frequently and successfully. But though some do it better than others, all of us are to do our part in telling the gospel.

4. Evangelism is preaching the gospel.

Evangelism simply means telling people the gospel. *Evangel* is the word for gospel. We evangelize when we tell someone the gospel. It is not sharing opinions, telling stories, sharing our testimony, singing songs, etc. We may tell the gospel through various means such as these, but the main thing is the message, not the method we may say it. We may tell it to a friend over coffee or in a Christmas letter, or we may share it by knocking on doors. We may tell it to close relatives, friends, acquaintances, or total strangers. Most people still have not heard the gospel. They may know some things about it, but not all the basic facts. The gospel is the basic account of the person and work of Jesus Christ for our salvation (1 Cor. 15:3–4).

5. We need to answer questions and objections.

We are to proclaim the gospel, but we are also to make sure that people understand us. Therefore, we are to explain, not just proclaim. It may mean answering people's questions. Some people haven't the slightest notion of how to get to Heaven. Others will try to argue with us. We need to give basic answers to everyone. Evangelism will then employ biblical apologetics to explain and defend the gospel. But we ought not to get sidetracked by secondary issues or become entangled in minor arguments. The main thing is to communicate the clear gospel.

6. The Bible is our guide to evangelism.

God saves the elect by means of the gospel (Rom. 10:17; 1 Peter 1:23). It is a seed that is to be sown everywhere (Matt. 13:3–8). God specifically uses His Word to save sinners. And the gospel is that part of the Word He uses to regenerate dead sinners (1 Peter 1:23–25). Our opinions or ideas do not mean anything. The Word is what counts. In fact, it is the simplicity of the Word that does it best, unencumbered by Madison Avenue techniques or other things. One good way to evangelize is to get someone to start reading the Bible. Also, we do biblical evangelism when we imitate those in the Bible, such as the apostle Paul, as they told the gospel to people no different from those we speak with.

7. We ought to refrain from gimmicks.

Just as we ought not to add to the gospel, so we ought not to do anything which would detract from the gospel or imply anything contrary to it. Most of modern evangelism is counterproductive. There is no biblical basis for things like altar calls, asking people to repeat "the sinner's prayer" after us, and other such gimmicks. One evangelist asked, "Why not? What harm could it do?" Such things do much harm by giving people false assurance that they are saved. "Easy believism" is a dangerous factory of false Christians. It leads millions to Hell and thus is one of the greatest enemies of true biblical evangelism.

8. We ought to have the right attitudes.

As we spread the gospel, we need to have attitudes that reflect the message we tell. We ought to have hearts of love for the lost (Rom. 9:1–3; 10:1; Mark 10:21). We should be serious. We ought to tremble at the awesome alternative for those who reject the gospel (2 Cor. 5:11). We need perseverance as we spread the gospel. Most people will not believe us. But don't lose heart. Some people will believe the gospel and will thank God forever that we were loving and brave enough to take the time to tell it to them. Above all, the main reason we spread the gospel is obedience to God. We tell the gospel so that God may be glorified.

9. Prayer is important to evangelism.

In evangelism, we speak to sinners on behalf of God. In prayer, we speak to God on behalf of sinners. We ought to pray for the lost to be saved (Rom. 10:1). First, pray for those to whom you have spoken. Then pray for those to whom you might be able to speak. And then those that others have spoken to. And then those to whom nobody has ever told the gospel. Pray also for fellow Christians who are spreading the gospel and that God would send out yet more laborers into His field (Matt. 9:38). Pray that God would stop the devil's opposition to our efforts. Plant the seeds, then water them with prayer.

10. We ought to support missionaries.

We ought to work in the corner of the vineyard in which God has placed us, but also support those in other corners. They go where we cannot go. One way to support them is by prayer. Another is financial gifts. Missionary work should be primarily evangelism, then church-planting. It may also include Bible translation and then discipleship teaching, and then other things such as medical missions. Christians should be compassionate in supporting missionaries, as well as sacrificial (2 Cor. 8:1–3) and wise. Missionaries are noble front-line soldiers who have sacrificed comfort back home to do what is often a thankless, hard, and dangerous job. We need to encourage them and pray for them. And maybe join them.

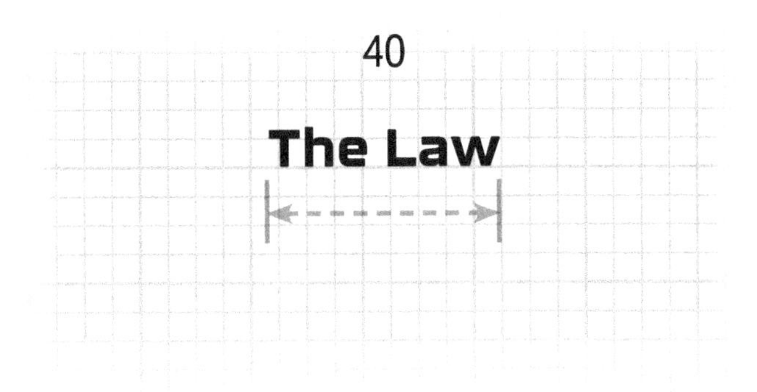

40

The Law

1. God gave us His law.

God gave His law to man to tell us our duty. Sin is defined as the breaking of this law (1 John 3:4). If there was no law, there would be no such thing as sin (Rom. 4:15). It is the "royal law" (James 2:8). The law is holy and just and good (Rom. 7:12). The Hebrew word for *law* is *torah*. The Greek word is *nomos*. God's law is given to all men through natural revelation (Rom. 2:14–15). It was given more specifically and verbally in the Bible.

2. The law is summarized in the Ten Commandments.

The Bible contains over six hundred laws in the Pentateuch alone, but God summarized them in the Ten Commandments, which are found in Exodus 20 and Deuteronomy 5. The first four commands deal with our relationship with God, and the next six with our relationship with other people. Some of them are negative; some are positive. When a certain thing is forbidden, its opposite is implicitly commanded. When something is commanded, its opposite is implicitly forbidden (see Eph. 4:28). Virtually every other law in the Bible is subsumed under these ten laws.

3. The law has three divisions.

When we study the many laws in the Bible, we find that they fall into three main categories. The *moral law* is the main one. The moral laws pertain to all men everywhere. They are written on our hearts and consciences. They predate Moses and continue today. They allow no exceptions. One might call these direct laws of pure morality. Others fall into the category of the *ceremonial law*. These are primarily ceremonial in nature and are only indirectly moral. They do not apply to all men, but only to those within the covenantal limits. For instance, Gentiles were never bound by the laws regarding circumcision, animal sacrifices or special festivals for the Jews. In the New Testament, non-Christians are not bound to keep baptism or the Lord's Supper. These laws are mainly types and symbols and are temporary. The third group are the *civil laws*, such as in Exodus 21–23. Some of these are meant to apply to all civil societies, such as capital punishment. Others were tied into the ceremonial laws and were temporary and only for Israel.

4. Part of the law has been changed.

Law as law cannot be changed any more than the very holy nature of God can be changed, for the law reflects that holiness. The moral law stands unalterable (see Matthew 5:17–19). Yet, God has changed the ceremonial law and the civil law in part. The Old Testament ceremonial laws were types of Christ, and so were fulfilled and abolished when Christ came (Col. 2:17). God then substituted these laws with two new ceremonies, namely baptism and Communion, which symbolize salvation with Christ as well. Those civil laws that had to do with Israel as a special theocracy have been abolished, while others of a purely moral nature still continue.

5. The law has three uses.

First, there is the political use. The law is meant to punish certain kinds of sinners (1 Tim. 1:9–10) and to act as a restraint on sin. Second, there is the pedagogical use. The law tells us what sin is, convicts of sin, and thus prepares us for conversion (Gal.3:24; Rom. 3:19–20; 7:7– 13). It silences all excuses and kills self-righteousness. Third, there is the didactic use. It teaches Christians how they may express gratitude to God for saving them (John 14:15, 21–24; 1 John 5:3).

6. Legalism is wrong.

There are two major misuses of the law. The first is *legalism*. It involves several things. Legalism is the religion of the Pharisees and Galatian Judaizers. It says we can be saved in whole or in part by law-keeping. Another form of legalism retains those Old Testament ceremonies which have passed away. Another form emphasizes the letter of the law over the Spirit of the law (2 Cor. 3:6). Another places human tradition on the same level. Another form puts more emphasis on law than on grace. But the Bible is clear: Christians are not under the curse of the law, nor under it as a means of salvation (Rom. 6:14–15). Christ has freed us from the dangers of legalism and warns us of it.

7. Antinomianism is wrong.

The opposite error from legalism is *antinomianism*. The word comes from the words *anti* (against) and *nomos* (law). It is an outlaw view of religion. It is similar to *libertinism* and *licentiousness*, which say that we have the liberty and license to sin all we want because we are not under the law but under grace. Doctrinal antinomianism says, "The law is one, therefore it has all been abolished" (the opposite of legalism, which says it has all been retained). It pretends to be super-spiritual by saying that the Spirit replaces the law. This is a false mysticism. It often advocates *situation ethics*. It sometimes says that works are totally unnecessary to the Christian, even as evidence of conversion. Most forms of dispensationalism teach a form of doctrinal antinomianism, claiming that the law was only for Israel and not the church.

8. The Holy Spirit enables us to keep the law.

The Spirit does not replace the law but leads the child of God to obey it. The spirit of the law does not annul the letter of the law. One of the great benefits of the new covenant is that the Spirit writes this law on our hearts and causes us to follow it (Jer. 31:33). In our state of sin, we could not keep the law. But being regenerate, we are freed from sin by the Spirit so that we can keep it, though never perfectly.

9. Christians should love God's law.

We ought to echo David's words, "Oh, how I love Your law!" (Ps. 119:97). Read through all of Psalm 119, the longest chapter in the Bible, and you'll see how David loved the law, did not forget it, learned from it, etc. Paul said, "I delight in the law" (Rom. 7:22). We show our love to God by loving His law. If we love Jesus, we will obey His law (John 14:15). We should obey it willingly and joyfully, not grudgingly. The law tells us how we may express our gratitude to God for saving us. Too many Christians have a low view of the law. To them, the law is bad, whereas God says the law is good and holy and perfect. It is sin, not the law, that is bad. The law stirs up the sin that is resident in us, but that doesn't make the law bad. The law by itself cannot save or move us to obedience. But it tells us the will of our heavenly Father.

10. The two love commands epitomize the law.

According to Matthew 22:37–39; Romans 13:9; Galatians 5:14; and James 2:8, the whole law is summed up in two simple laws: Love God and love other people. This is the heart of the law. It is a summary. A table of contents does not annul the rest of the book, but indexes it. So too here. Love is the inner attitude that shows true obedience to the meaning of the law. God desires us to love Him with all our being. God also tells us to love other people as Jesus loved us, even to love our enemies. The law truly is a law of love.

41

The Progress of Redemption

1. God worked progressively in history.

God's eternal plan was worked out over many years in history. The Bible begins "In the beginning" and ends in eternity future. In between, God is at work. He has worked progressively by stages, each building on the previous, like building a house on a foundation. It had to be like this. Christ did not come before Adam, nor immediately after Adam and Eve sinned. He came as Savior, which meant that sin had to happen first. And the way had to be made ready for the coming of Christ. He came in "the fullness of the time" (Gal. 4:4), in the center of history. This progression is sometimes called *Holy History*. It is like the growth of a child to maturity or the rising of a sun to full strength.

2. God sent prophets to prepare for Christ.

Hebrews 1:1–2 says that God spoke through many ways and finally in Christ. History is the stage for a progression of revelation of God. One way in which God spoke progressively was through a series of prophets. Like

John the Baptist, the last of the Old Testament prophets, they prepared the way for the coming of Christ. They all spoke to people in their own day, but also pointed to the future when God's goal would be reached. Some spoke of the first coming, others of the second, still others of both. But they all spoke about Christ (Acts 10:43; Luke 24:25–27, 44). Some spoke of His person, some of His work, some of both. History is Christocentric.

3. People were saved by believing in the coming Messiah.

The gospel was revealed in various ways in the periods of time before Christ. The many symbols of the temple all prefigured Christ, especially the sacrifices (Heb. 9:9; 10:1; Col. 2:17). But it was especially the prophecies that gave the gospel, starting with the very first one in Genesis 3:15. Abraham, Moses, and many others were saved by believing in the coming Messiah who would defeat Satan, provide the perfect sacrifice, and reconcile them to God. The gospel was not nearly as clear then as now. But they were not saved merely by believing that God would give them land, children, etc.

4. Salvation has always been by grace through faith.

A common mistake is to think that people in the Old Testament were saved by keeping the law. Or that they were to obey as much as they could and offer a sacrifice for sin to make up the rest. Romans 4 kills this heresy. Abraham was justified by faith, not works. So was David. It has always been by God's sheer grace. And the condition has always been the same: faith. It has never been by works. Nor has it been by nationality. Though the Jews had special privileges, they were saved by grace, not by race. The same is true today regarding Christians and their children. God has always had only one way of salvation: His way. And it centers in Christ.

5. Grace and law are in both Testaments.

Another common error is to suppose that the Old Testament was all law and no grace and the New Testament is all grace and no law. Actually, both are in both. There is simply more emphasis on one than the other in each. One cannot read the Old Testament without finding the great Hebrew word *hesed*—covenantal love, free mercy, grace. Similarly, we find law in the New Testament as well. Otherwise, one would have to conclude Old Testament people were saved by law and that there is no law in the New Testament—both very dangerous errors. John 1:17 says that Moses gave the law and that Christ gave grace. But this does not mean that Christ did not give grace before He came. He gave it to those who believed He would come. And the law has gone from Moses' hand to Christ's.

6. God used Israel in a special way

Just as God flooded the whole world and started over with Noah and his family, so God started something new with Abraham and his family. They were to be a special nation dedicated to God. Not superior to Gentiles, Israel was to be a light to the nations and bring God's blessings to them. God made Israel a special theocracy, something He has not done for any other nation. They were even given a specific land grant. But there were conditions to all this, which Israel did not keep. Some of the promises to the seed of Abraham were fulfilled in national Israel in the Old Testament; others have been fulfilled in the church; but they are mainly centered in Christ (Gal. 3). God's program for Israel was good but failed because of the deficiencies of human nature. Israel was at the heart of most of the Old Testament. All that time, God let the Gentiles at large go their own way (Acts 14:16). Eventually Israel ended up as bad as them.

7. Israel and the church are related but not identical.

In my view, Israel and the church are not two separate entities, as taught by dispensationalism. Nor are they entirely the same, nor does the church entirely take Israel's place, as taught by *covenant theology*. The truth is in the middle. Some Old Testament promises to Israel are fulfilled in physical Israel, some in the church. The two groups overlap. In one sense, Israel was the church in an embryonic form. Acts 7:38 (KJV) even calls it the "church in the wilderness." On the other hand, the church is the true or mature Israel, called "the Israel of God" in Galatians 6:16. Still, there was a sense in which the church didn't begin properly until Acts 2. Similarly, there is a sense in which Israel, as Israel, continues. Romans 11 talks about God's one tree, not two separate trees. There is one body, not two.

8. God made a series of covenants.

All of God's dealings with man are covenantal. A covenant is a contract, an agreement between two or more parties, with promises and conditions. The first covenant was the covenant of works with Adam as representative for all men. Adam broke it and sinners are still under its curse. God made another covenant with Noah and his family, which also failed. Then there was the covenant with Abraham, with a later subsection added through Moses. Israel failed to keep this covenant, too. There were also several individual covenants, such as with David. Each of these marked a new stage in God's dealings with man. Each ended in failure. But each also laid the foundation for a fulfillment of them all through the last and greatest of all the covenants.

9. Jesus Christ made the new covenant.

Just as all God's dealings with men are covenantal and are through Christ, the perfect revelation of God, so it was fitting that Christ would make the greatest covenant of all. It was predicted here and there in the Old Testament, especially Jeremiah 31:31–34, and was sealed in Christ's blood. Unlike the others, this one is perfect and unbreakable. It is the Covenant of covenants. God keeps His part and guarantees that we keep ours, for in one sense Christ has kept all the conditions on our side for us. This fulfills and supersedes all the previous ones.

10. Christ inaugurated the kingdom of God.

Another key feature to God's progressive plan is the kingdom of God. In one sense, God rules over all things. In another, Israel was meant to be the kingdom. In another, believers have always been in it. Christ the King brought it in and is now expanding it through the church. One day, the plan of history will be fulfilled when the Messiah King returns.

42

The Universal Church

1. The church is God's special people.

All people belong to God because He is their Creator. But in a more important sense, there is a select group that is God's special people. They are called the church. The word *church* is *ecclesia* in Greek. It means "gathering, assembly, congregation, group." It consists of those who have been "called out." We were initially called out by election, then in our conversion. It is called "the church of God" (Acts 20:28). Christ called it "My church" (Matt. 16:18).

2. The universal church includes all true believers.

All believers and only believers are in this church. We call it the *universal church* not because it includes all men everywhere but because it includes believers from every tribe, nation, and language (Rev. 5:9). It includes men and women, young and old, rich and poor, slave and free, intellectuals and uneducated (1 Cor. 12:13). We also refer to it as the *invisible church* because it is not limited to any one place. The theory of *landmarkism* says there is only the local visible church, not a universal invisible church. But the New Testament speaks of this church in the collective singular (as in Matt. 16:18) as well as in the individual plural (such as churches of Galatia [Gal. 1:2]). Unbelievers may belong to the local church but are not part of the true universal church.

3. The church is not any one denomination.

The Roman Catholic Church claims to be the only true church. Many cults make the same claim. The fact is that those groups are not part of the true church at all because they teach heresy. Nor is the true church limited to any one denomination that is true in doctrine. Some Landmark Baptists think that theirs is the only true church because it is in the chain-link going back to John the Baptist and Christ. This is the same error of *apostolic succession* as in Catholicism, namely, that the true church is one denomination and must be in an organized union going back to the New Testament. But the true church is a spiritual organism, not a manmade organization. The universal church has members in a variety of denominations, and no one group is the one and only church.

4. True church unity is in Christ.

Christ prayed for His church to be one (John 17). But how is this accomplished? Not through one denomination, nor through the ecumenical movement, which throws out the gospel and brings in heresy. Rather, true unity is by Christ Himself. It is brought about by the Holy Spirit, fostered by love and protected by peaceful relations between Christians. This is one of the main themes of Ephesians. This unity is not to be seen in "Christendom," which includes all churches and people who give the broadest and vaguest professions of being Christian. By far most of them are not part of the true church at all, for they are not united to Christ in a spiritual way.

5. The church is not a cult.

Ecumenism is too inclusive—it includes far too many people in the church. The cults are too exclusive—they exclude too many. Actually, neither are part of the true church. Cults are united, not by Christ or the Spirit or the truth, but by a charismatic leader, antisocial tendencies among their members, weird practices or heresies, and other unbiblical things. The true church is related to Christ and is not cultic.

6. The church is the house of God.

God uses a variety of metaphors to describe the church. One is that the church is a house (Eph. 3:15). Paul, in Ephesians, describes it like this: Christ is the chief cornerstone, the apostles and prophets are the foundation, and believers are individual bricks which are connected to each other by the Spirit and love (Eph. 4:3). We are to edify each other, and thereby build up the church (1 Cor. 14:12). A local church may meet in a building, but the church consists of people, not wood or metal or bricks. We are the house of God.

7. The church is the family of God.

God also likens His people to a family (Eph. 3:15). God is the Father, Christ is our older brother, and we are brothers and sisters of each other (Mark 3:35). There are no grandchildren in this family. One enters this family by the new birth, not physical birth. One does not enter it because his physical parents are in it. One day, the entire family will be together in Heaven. This special family is more important than our physical family, for natural relations are for this life only. It is the blood of Christ, not parental or racial blood, that runs through this family.

8. The church is the body of Christ.

Another popular way to describe the church is to liken it to a human body. This is discussed in Ephesians, Colossians, 1 Corinthians 12, Romans 12, and elsewhere. Christ is the head of the body (Eph. 1:22–23). Note two things. First, Christ is the *only* head. The Catholic pope claims to be the head, but that would make the church a monster with two heads. Nor is any king the head. In some countries (e.g., England), the reigning monarch claims to be the head of the church. No one but Christ is the head of the universal or even the local church. Second, Christ has only one body (Eph. 4:4). He is not the head of false bodies like Islam or Buddhism. Each Christian is a member of this body and needs all other members and should minister to others.

9. The church is the bride of Christ.

A very dear metaphor for the church is the figure of it being the very bride of Jesus Christ (Eph. 5:25). Christ never married any one woman—let alone many, as taught by Mormonism. Rather, He is married to each and every true believer. Roman Catholicism teaches that nuns are special brides of Christ, but that too is wrong. He is married to all believers collectively and to each believer personally. The order is this: we were betrothed to Christ in eternity, engaged to Him in conversion, and will be finally united to Him in the consummation of heavenly marriage after the second coming (Rev. 19:7; 21:2). In the Old Testament, Israel was meant to be the bride of God but proved to be adulterous (Jeremiah 3; Ezekiel 16; Hosea 2–4). The true remnant of Israel was part of the bride of Christ, for this bride is a spiritual and not a national or physical bride. God has one bride, not two. Therefore, true Israel and the church form the one bride.

10. The church is the temple of God.

There are many other wonderful metaphors for this great people of God called the church, but none is so wonderful as that of it being the temple of God (Eph. 2:21). In one sense, the entire universe is a temple of God's glory. In another sense, Israel was meant to be it. Then there was the tabernacle and, next, the temple. These were all preparatory to Christ, who Himself is the final temple (John 2:21; Rev. 21:22). We are united to Christ and thereby become part of this temple. A temple is where God shows His special glory and presence. God is everywhere but especially in and among His people who are united to Christ. Each of us is a temple of the Spirit (1 Cor. 6:19), and together we form this great temple. Our main purpose is to be the place where God shows His glory and where we reflect it back to Him in worship. This is true in each locality and perfectly fulfilled one day in Heaven.

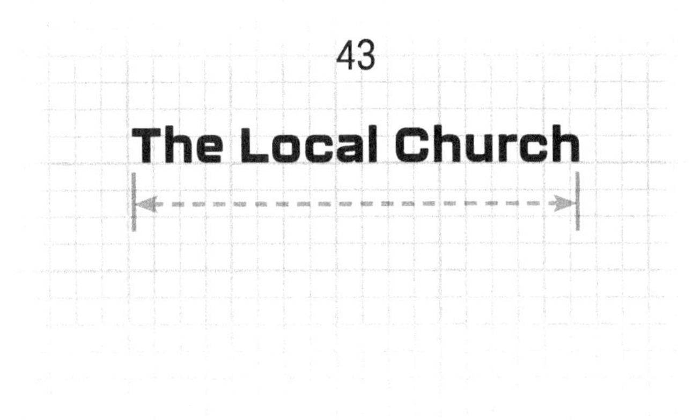

43 The Local Church

1. The local church is part of the universal church.

The local church is that visible part of the invisible church in a given locality. It does not include every believer in the world, only a few. It is part of the larger group, just as each believer is part of the church at large. In one way, the two should match each other. All members of the universal church should be members of a local church (sadly, some are not, Heb. 10:25). Conversely, all who are members of the local church should be members of the universal church (sadly, many are not). Just as there was an Israel within Israel (Rom. 9:6, 27), so there is a church within the church, as it were. The New Testament speaks of local churches in Ephesus, Colossae, etc., localized by cities, and not nations, class, race, etc.

2. The main purpose of the local church is worship.

Worship is the prime directive, the *raison d'être*, our reason for existence. This is true of both the universal and the local church. A local body does not exist for good things which are not essential, such as potluck suppers. Some New Testament churches engaged in a meal called the *agape* (1 Cor. 10–11). It could be useful but was to be canceled if detrimental to essential purposes of the church. Nor is charity our main purpose for being. We exist here for the same reason we will in Heaven: worship. Nothing should hinder this purpose or detract from it. Worship is not "having a good time." It is not fun, entertainment, or emotionalism. It is the reception and reflection of God's glory. It is meant to please God, not us. Any local church that does not worship God is failing in its purpose. If it doesn't get back on track, it should close its doors. Each Christian can and should worship God alone everywhere, but especially together in the church.

3. Worship is to be regulated by the Word of God.

God tells us how He will be worshiped, and He tells us how in the Bible alone (Col. 2:23; Matt. 15:9). He does not leave it to our imaginations, for we are prone to idolatry, the very opposite of worship. Nor does He leave it to majority vote, fads or fashions, or what is popular at the moment, and He does not allow us to borrow from pagan forms of worship. We call this the *regulative principle of worship*. God is not pleased with our inventions or gimmicks. On the other hand, true biblical worship is pleasing to God. God will reveal His glory to His people only through biblical means and, in turn, will receive only biblical worship. Done properly, worship is spiritually uplifting, not boring. It is the very vestibule of Heaven on earth. We should therefore strive to follow it.

4. The church is to build up its members.

This is the second main priority of the local church. We are to edify one another, individually and collectively (Eph. 4:15–16). We can do this through fellowship, use of our spiritual gifts, encouragement, charity, and other means. When the church comes together, the main means by which it is edified individually and collectively is through the faithful preaching of the Word of God. All members are to be involved in the work of mutual edification. The strong have a special responsibility to help the weak (Rom. 15:1). By ministering to each other, we minister to Christ (Matt. 25:34–40).

5. The church is to preach the gospel.

This is the third major purpose of the local church. All Christians are to spread the gospel. But there is a sense in which we are to do it together (prayer, encouragement, etc.). Without it, we get lazy and fat and self-centered. With evangelism, we retain spiritual vitality.

6. All Christians should belong to a local church.

Membership in a local church is not an optional extra. It is commanded by God. Failure to do so is rebuked in Hebrews 10:25. We all need to be members of a local body, under the guidance of God-ordained elders (Heb. 13:17), accountable to them and the body. God permits no "lone ranger" believers. We are sheep that need to be in a flock with shepherds. We are to be members of a team. We may shop around for a while to find a good one within a reasonable distance, but there is a difference between church-shopping and church-hopping. We are to be members, too, not merely guests. And one can belong to only one local church at a time.

7. Only Christians may belong to a local church.

Just as there are only true saints in the universal church, there ought to be only true believers in each local church. The Bible teaches a "believers-only membership." A candidate needs to give a valid profession of faith, including evidence of being born again and an acceptance of the basics of the gospel. A membership that is part Christian, part non-Christian is a recipe for eventual disaster. Israel in the wilderness was a mixed multitude, and their problems often began with the Egyptians who tagged along. Unbelievers are to be removed from the membership roll but are to be encouraged to attend.

8. A church should have one main weekly meeting.

The weekly main meeting is described under the phrase "when you come together" in 1 Corinthians 10, 11, and 14. God has always had an appointed time and place of worship for His people. Today, it is the local church meeting on the Lord's Day (Acts 20:7; 1 Cor. 16:2). The main duty is not merely to refrain from work on the Sabbath but to worship with God's people. Much of the pattern of the meeting of the New Testament local church was patterned after the meetings of the Jewish synagogue (James 2:2). Attendance at these meetings is mandatory, not optional. All Christians should attend and participate, unless providentially hindered by legitimate reasons (illness, being out of town, in jail, works of mercy, etc.). Sadly, too many saints allow sports, family visitors, rest from Saturday activities, TV shows, and other such trivia to keep them from what God commands for their good.

9. The weekly meeting includes several activities.

The Bible mentions several things that are essential to this weekly meeting. One is the reading of the Scriptures (Col. 4:16). Another is the public preaching and teaching of the Bible by a gifted man (not woman) (1 Cor. 14:34–35; 1 Tim. 2:11–12). Then there is prayer (1 Tim. 2:18; Matt. 21:13); the singing of hymns (1 Cor. 14:26); evangelism; fellowship; weekly Communion (Acts 20:7; 1 Cor. 10–11); the use of spiritual gifts (1 Cor. 14); baptism; the collection (1 Cor. 16:2); and perhaps one or two others. Forbidden are things which are not in Scripture. There is liberty within biblical lines as to how the legitimate functions may take place (who, how long, what order, etc.).

10. The church should strive to conform to God's ideal.

No local church is perfect. All need improvement. Occasionally God may send revival. We can pray for it and repent of anything that hinders it, but only God can send it. On the other hand, we can and must work hard for true reformation. We need to be "reformed and always reforming" so as better to conform to God's ideal as laid down in the Bible. No church has the luxury of coasting, nor of being defeated by lethargy. It is Christ's church and it is our privilege and duty to be in it and work for it to His glory.

44

Church Government

1. The local church should be independent.

God has ordained each local church as an entity in itself. There is no warrant in the Bible for denominations. Indeed, passages such as 1 Corinthians 1 would forbid denominations. A local church should be friendly with other local churches. They can cooperate in a variety of things. But there is to be no outside authority. The only exception to this was in the days of the apostles. But there are no more apostles. The council in Acts 15 was supervised by apostles. Any council today may be useful for consultation but can carry no authority. Thus, there are no denominations, headquarters, official canons, or the like in the New Testament.

2. Church and state are separate.

God has ordained three basic institutions: the family, the state, and the church. None may encroach upon the sphere of the others. The kingdom of the state may not exert authority in the church. The theory of Erastianism says that the reigning monarch is the head of the church, as in England. But the Bible does not permit state churches. Nor does it permit church states, such as a theocracy (except for Old Testament Israel). State citizenship cannot equal church membership. Taxes and tithes are different. The state must not persecute the church. It has the power of the sword over criminals, but not the power of the Word over Christians. Nor is the pope over either state or church. Christians may and should be involved in state functions as good citizens, but church and state must be distinct kingdoms. Neither rules the other.

3. The Bible is the final authority in the church.

Creeds, confessions of faith, catechisms, and constitutions are useful. But they are not final. Only the Bible is final. Tradition ("the way we've always done things around here") is also subject to the Bible. Catholicism reverses all this by placing the authority of the church over that of Scripture. The only authority any church or officer has is through the Word of God. No pastor is the "king of the congregation." Only Christ is King, and He rules by His word.

4. Church constitutions are useful.

Though not the final authority, church constitutions can indeed serve a useful purpose. They state exactly where a local church officially stands on certain doctrines and practices. Otherwise, church government easily degenerates into mob rule. Many groups, especially some cults, say they have no constitution. Some "Brethren" churches also disdain constitutions. But upon further investigation, most have some sort of written agreement. Secret documents are dangerous, so a church constitution should be open for all to read.

5. Church government is neither democratic nor dictatorial.

The local church is not a pure democracy, in which every person has the same vote as everybody else.

That idea is from pagan Greece, not the Bible. It is even questionable whether members are allowed to vote at all, except on the choice of deacons (Acts 6:3–5). What if a majority of new believers outnumbered the mature believers, and took over and went off onto strange fads? Children don't rule their parents. Members are to follow their leaders (Heb. 13:7, 17, 24). The leaders are not to be dictators, but to imitate the loving serving leadership of Christ (1 Peter 5:2–3).

6. Elders are ordained by God to rule the church.

God has chosen to raise up those who are called elders (Acts 20:17; 1 Peter 5:1–2). The word for *elder* is *presbuteros*, from which we get the word *presbyter*. Originally the word meant an older man who exerted authority by reason of the wisdom of his years. Later, it came to refer to a local magistrate or alderman. In the New Testament, it refers to those who are God-ordained to exert authority in the local church. They rule by the Word. They need not be older, but neither should they be new converts or children (1 Tim. 3:6). In addition to spiritual maturity, 1 Timothy 3 and Titus 1 list many other requisite qualifications. They are to be men, not women (1 Tim. 2:11).

7. Elders, pastors, and bishops are the same.

Two other important terms are used to describe this office. One is the word *pastor*, which means "shepherd" (Eph. 4:11). Actually, he is an under-shepherd, under the Chief Shepherd (1 Peter 5:4). Shepherds are to look after the sheep (Ps. 23; Acts 20:28), that is, members of their local flock. They are to provide food and water (the Word of God), tend to their personal needs (like counselling, visitation, encouragement), warn them of danger (rebuke, church discipline, warning of wolves, etc.), and so on. Then there is the word *bishop*, used in

Titus 1 and elsewhere. This is not someone in authority over the pastors of many local churches, as taught by Rome, Episcopalianism, Methodism, and others. A bishop is simply an overseer, a superintendent, a leader. It is the same office as pastor and elder.

8. There are no priests, cardinals, or popes in Scripture.

The Bible gives elders and deacons, but no other officers. Every believer is a priest (Rev. 1:6; 1 Peter 2:9). There is no separate office for priest or vicar in the New Testament comparable to the priests or Levites in the Old Testament. Bishops are elders. There isn't even the slightest hint of anything like cardinals in the Bible. And the only parallel to the idea of pope in Scripture is the one who sets himself above the church of God claiming rights for himself which belong to Christ alone (2 Thess. 2:4). There was a high priest in the Old Testament, but the New Testament fulfillment is Christ, not the pope (Heb. 3:1). Nor are there other offices, such as the prophet (as in Mormonism). Some churches say they have apostles, but the biblical apostles had a unique office. The only apostles that continue are simply missionaries.

9. Elders are equal in authority.

The Bible teaches that there should be a plurality of elders in each local church (Acts 20:17; 1 Peter 5:1). This is a safeguard against any one pastor from having too much authority. A lone authority is easily corrupted (2 John 9). One or more elders may serve full time and be financially paid by the church (1 Tim. 5:17–18), but they have no more authority than the others. Elders are thus accountable to each other. Together they form a team of leadership and service.

10. Deacons are servants of the church.

Elders are to rule, deacons are to serve. Deacons do not have authority. Yet they are to be highly qualified and spiritually mature (1 Tim. 3:8–13; Acts 6:3). They are not as essential to the church as elders. Still, they fill a very useful place in the ongoing work of the local church. Their major work is to tend to the physical needs of church members, such as the poor, ill, and elderly (Acts 6:1–2). Maintenance of church property and finances are also their job. It would seem from passages like Luke 8:2–3 and 1 Timothy 3:11 that women may serve as deaconesses, especially in areas of service to other women (especially widows) and where women are naturally more gifted than men. Elders are selected by elders, deacons by the whole church under the approval of the elders.

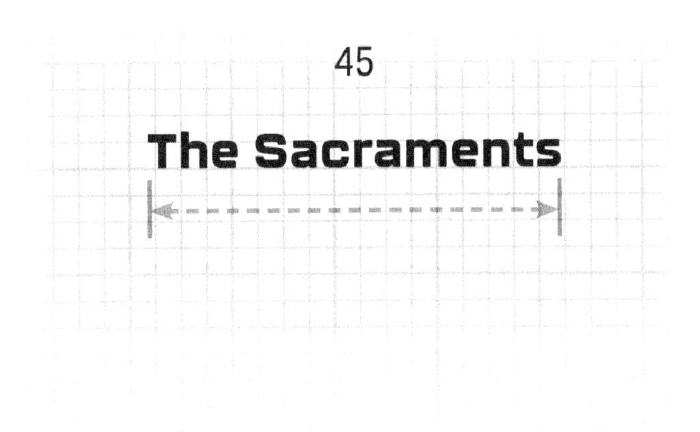

45

The Sacraments

1. God has always given His people religious ceremonies.

God has always had a people. He has always commanded them to worship Him. God has always given them distinct ways in which to worship Him. God has always provided them with ceremonies which are fitting to their point in time. For instance, Old Testament worship was very elaborate in the temple. It included incense, animal sacrifices, priestly garments, etc. It was very detailed and prescribed. Yet God's approved ceremonies have always been mainly symbolic in nature. These are called *sacraments* because they are holy ceremonies. They are also called *ordinances*, for they are ordained by God.

2. The New Testament ceremonies replace the Old Testament ceremonies.

Most of the Old Testament ceremonies revolved around animal sacrifices in the temple. These prefigured Christ. When the sun rose, the shadows fled away. We do not need sacrifices, altars, and priests any longer. Circumcision was another Old Testament sacrament, a badge that one was a member of Israel. It has been replaced by baptism, with several modifications (it is only for believers, women and not just men, etc.) Most, if not all, New Testament ceremonies symbolize the same things that had been prefigured in the Old Testament ceremonies. Circumcision is now needless, except possibly for medical purposes. The New Testament ceremonies are far fewer and far simpler than in the Old Testament, for New Testament worship is more spiritual.

3. There are only two sacraments.

The Catholic Church says there are seven (baptism, Mass, confirmation, penance, holy orders, marriage, last rites), but the New Testament knows only two. There is no sacrament of confirmation, nor penance. Ministerial ordination is biblical but is not quite a sacrament. Laying on of hands and prayer for the sick are biblical (Mark 16:18), as is anointing with oil (James 5:14), but again, these are not quite sacraments. Some churches feel that foot-washing is a sacrament, but it seems rather to be an optional practice like the *agape* (love feast) or just a practical service to others. Other groups, such as the Salvation Army and some ultra-dispensational groups, think that baptism and Communion are no longer valid. But Christ ordained them for the church until He returns (1 Cor. 11:26; Matt. 28:19–20).

4. The sacraments are not magic.

Sacraments are primarily symbolic in nature. They do not automatically confer grace or spiritual benefits *ex opere operato*, like if we say the magic words or wave our hands in the right way. That is what is called magic and is pagan in nature. The Bible teaches that we are to practice the sacraments, but we need to beware of the overemphasis on them found in some churches. We must resist the lure of sacralism, sacramentalism, sacerdotalism, liturgicalism, and other forms of magic and priest-craft. The true spiritual power is in the word by the Spirit. Nevertheless, we should not go to the opposite extreme in devaluing them.

5. Water baptism in the first sacrament.

The first sacrament for which a Christian is eligible is baptism in water. Ideally, it should be done by total immersion (Matt. 3:16; John 3:23). It need not be by "trine" immersion (dipping three times). The use of the name of the Trinity is important (Matt. 28:19) but is not a magic formula. Baptism symbolizes cleansing from sin (Acts 22:16), union with Christ (Gal. 3:27), identification with His death and resurrection (Rom. 6:3–4), and the inner baptism with the Holy Spirit (Matt. 3:11).

6. Baptism is for believers only.

All the commands for baptism lay down the condition of faith/repentance. Infants and unbelievers do not meet this condition any more than bells or horses, and so are not eligible. Nearly every example in the New Testament shows that the one being baptized was a believer. The overwhelming pattern is clear: faith must precede baptism. There are no commands nor examples of infants being baptized. Infant baptism usually is associated with baptismal regeneration. Even in churches that deny baptismal regeneration, they tend to presume that the baby is/has been/will be regenerated somehow. This is leftover baggage from Roman Catholicism. Infant baptism manufactures millions of false Christians and sends them to Hell with false assurance.

7. Baptism follows salvation.

One who comes to faith in Christ and is saved is commanded to be baptized. Ideally this should be done soon thereafter (Acts 2:41; 16:33). But it is important to realize that water baptism in no shape or form produces salvation. The thief on the cross died unbaptized (Luke 23:40–43). Simon Magus was baptized but was never saved (Acts 8:13–23). Baptismal regeneration is a dangerous heresy taught by Rome, Episcopalianism, Lutheranism, the Church of Christ, the Christian Church, the Disciples of Christ, many cults, Greek Orthodoxy, and others. Some say it doesn't produce salvation, it only completes it. Others say it infuses saving grace which needs to be cultivated or else will be lost. Whatever form it takes, it is heresy of the first order. Salvation is totally by grace through faith by the word and Spirit, not by water.

8. The Lord's Supper is the second sacrament.

The second holy ordinance is variously called the Lord's Supper, the Lord's Table, Communion, or the Eucharist. It is mainly symbolic in nature, typifying the death and resurrection of Christ (1 Cor. 11:23–26). The bread and wine do not change, as supposed in the Catholic heresy of the Mass. Nor do they automatically infuse grace. Ideally, the New Testament order is: conversion → baptism → Communion. But one wonders if we should refuse Communion to a born-again believer who has not yet been baptized. The Supper basically replaces all the Old Testament sacrifices, especially Passover.

9. The Lord's Supper is for believers only.

There are conditions for the proper taking of Communion which exclude infants and unbelievers: self-examination (1 Cor. 11:28), faith, repentance, remembering Christ (Luke 22:19), discerning the body (1 Cor. 11:29). The idea of infant Communion is unbiblical, superstitious, and dangerous. Communion is for all believers, except those who have been excommunicated from a local church. Unbelievers and backslidden believers should be warned not to partake (1 Cor. 11:27–32).

10. The Lord's Supper is a special time of communion with Christ.

The Supper is symbolic, but not merely symbolic. It is a time to renew one's faith in the Lord Jesus, draw near to Him in prayer, and commune with Him heart-to-heart in deepest spiritual intimacy. The classic verse here is 1 Corinthians 10:16. The spiritual experience is not magically produced by the elements or a priest, but by the Holy Spirit through means of the word of God. Appropriate Scripture ought to be read at each Communion. First Corinthians 10 and 11 also makes it an integral part of the weekly meeting of the church. It ought to be practiced in a holy and worthy manner, seriously and joyfully, looking back to the cross and forward to the second coming of our Lord.

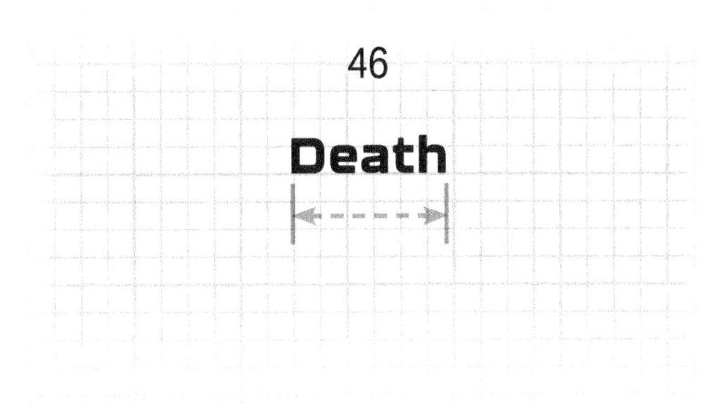

1. All of us will die.

Death is an important and serious subject. It ought not to be ignored or laughed at. Everyone will die sooner or later. Some die young, some old; some by accidents, some by illness. Death is no respecter of persons. Only two people entered this world in an unusual way (Adam and Eve) and only two people left it without dying (Enoch and Elijah). Even Mary and the apostles all died. Only Christians who are alive at the time of the second coming will escape death (1 Cor. 15:51). The genealogies in Genesis frequently say, "So-and-so lived so many years and he died." People have devised all sorts of ways to avoid death. None have been successful.

2. Death is the result of sin.

"The wages of sin is death" (Rom. 6:23). We earned death. We have a death penalty on us. "The soul who sins shall die" (Ezek. 18:4). God told Adam that he would die if he sinned (Gen. 2:17). If Adam had never sinned, he never would have died. Through him, sin and death entered the world (Rom. 5:12). Even Christians die, for we still have original sin in us. Sin brings death like conception brings life (James 1:15).

3. The soul leaves the body at death.

There are a variety of ways in which scientists and doctors have tried to define death. The most popular is that death is when all brain waves totally cease. That may be the best biological answer. But there is a more important definition. According to the Bible, death occurs when the soul leaves the body (Gen. 35:18). "The body without the spirit is dead" (James 2:26). Jesus died by voluntarily yielding His spirit into the Father's hands (Luke 23:46). The body will turn to dust, while the spirit returns to face God (Eccl. 12:7). The soul enters at conception and leaves at death.

4. There is no reincarnation or second chance.

There are many false ideas about what happens at death and after death. The Bible alone is our only sure guide. One of the most popular errors about death is that it opens the door to a new life via reincarnation. The idea comes from Hinduism and Buddhism, not the Bible. Hebrews 9:27 says that it is appointed for us once to die, and then judgment day follows. Our doom is sealed at death. There is no second chance after death. Sinners do not get to hear the gospel in the next world, nor are they sent back here for another shot at being a good person. God has occasionally raised a person from the dead, but even they later died.

5. Death is both an enemy and a friend.

Death comes as either an enemy or a friend, depending on whether that person is ready to meet God. Death is called an "enemy" in 1 Corinthians 15:26. It was not a part of the original creation. Sinners may mock death, but when it arrives, they will be terrified. The death angel will be sent by God to strike sinners dead at their appointed time (Isa. 37:36). He will take no excuses or bribes; his errand is always accomplished. On the other hand, God sends angels to usher the souls of dying Christians to Heaven (Luke 16:22). All pain will be past; only pleasure awaits us. In this sense, death is a friend to believers. Thomas Goodwin, the Puritan, said before he died, "He whom I feared as an enemy has come as a beloved friend." Psalm 116:15 says, "Precious in the sight of the LORD is the death of His saints."

6. The souls of the dead are conscious.

There are many false ideas about what happens after death. One is that the souls of the dead cease to exist. That is the devil's lie. Another false notion is that souls are alive but unconscious. This is the theory called "soul sleep." It, too, is wrong. The souls of both saints and sinners are wide awake. The metaphor of sleep is applied to their bodies, not their spirits (John 11:11–13). Their bodies sleep in the grave, in the sense that they will one day be awakened at their future resurrection (1 Cor. 15). The story of the rich man and Lazarus in Luke 16 clearly tells us that both Christians and non-Christians are wide awake and fully conscious after death. This is the mysterious realm of the *intermediate state*, which is that period between individual death and final destiny.

7. Believers go immediately to paradise.

The very moment a believer dies, his soul goes to be with Christ. The dying thief went to paradise (Luke 23:43). Sometimes this place is called Abraham's bosom (Luke 16:22) or the third Heaven (2 Cor. 12:2, 4). It is Heaven as it is now, not the new Heaven that is yet future. It is perfect bliss and peace, for we are with God. The Bible says that we go to be "with the Lord" when we die (2 Cor. 5:8; Phil. 1:23). Their bodies are still back on earth, their souls in glory.

8. There is no purgatory.

The Catholic Church teaches that believers first go to a place of preparation called *purgatory*, a place of fire and torment in which sins are burned out of us to purge us of all original sin and its taint. People supposedly stay there for varying lengths of time, some running into thousands of years. But all make it to Heaven, and so purgatory is said to be a blessing. But none of this is taught in the Bible. Christians go immediately to be with Christ—is Christ in purgatory? We go to immediate happiness—is there joy in torment? All sin and its effects are left in our bodies in the grave. Our souls are immediately freed from the presence of sin and we are made perfect in a moment (Heb. 12:23). Only the blood of Christ cleanses from sin (1 John 1:7).

9. Unbelievers immediately go to Hades.

Those who die in their sins go straight to Hades (Luke 16:23). This is the present state of Hell, not the future form called *gehenna*. Sinners are there in their souls, not their bodies, which are still on earth. Hades is a place of fiery torment (Luke 16:23–24). But it is temporary, not permanent. It is the holding place for sinners until they go before God at the last judgment (Rev. 20:13). This does not mean that their final doom is uncertain. No one in Hades will ever make it to Heaven, nor will anyone in paradise make it to eternal Hell. The intermediate states match the final ends.

10. We should be prepared to die.

Since death is inevitable and can come at any time, it is vitally important that we all be ready to die. But because death leads us to God and judgment, sinners have devised many alternative theories. One popular idea today is the nonsense of "out of body experiences," in which a person supposedly dies, sees a bright light, has great peace, then reenters his body, never to fear death again. It is a lie of the devil. Death is a rude awakening to reality. Believers need to get their houses in order, too (Isa. 38:1). And we need to warn unbelievers of their doom and tell them the only way to escape the penalty for sin. We need to invite them to come to Heaven with us.

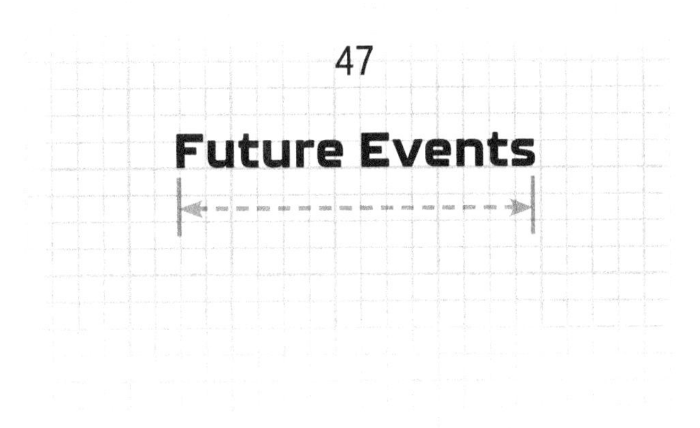

47

Future Events

1. Good and evil will continue.

God foreordained the future and knows what will happen. He has revealed some of these events to us in advance. The parable of the weeds in Matthew 13 tells us that weeds will grow in the field with the wheat until the harvest. That is, there will be unbelievers and believers in the world until the end. Some Christians optimistically think that Christianity will be so successful that there will be virtually no unbelievers left when Christ returns. Others think the opposite—there will be almost no Christians left. The truth is that both will continue.

2. There will be a great revival of Jews coming to Christ.

Romans 11 describes a significant aspect of how the world will continue until the second coming. God promised that many of Abraham's descendants would be blessed and through them the whole world would be blessed. The primary fulfillment of this is through Christ (Gal. 3). Then there is the way in which the church fulfills this as the spiritual children of Abraham. There is yet a third way this will be fulfilled. One day, God will stir up large numbers of Jews to a kind of spiritual envy as they reclaim Jesus as their Messiah. Many, perhaps most, Jews will become Christians. In turn, this will stir up the Gentiles at large to come to Christ in large numbers. This has not yet happened but must happen before Christ returns. In this way, the Abrahamic covenant is fulfilled through Christ and the new covenant. Israel will not be specially blessed merely because of race, but by faith in Christ.

3. There will be a time of great persecution.

Various texts predict that persecution will continue to the end. We have seen periods of greater and lesser persecution. Many scholars interpret some of these texts as predicting a time of great tribulation, in which Christians are severely persecuted right before the end. Much of the question revolves around Matthew 24. Some think this refers to the siege of Jerusalem in AD 70; others see it as all future; still others as both; and yet others as symbolic of church history in general. The best answer is that there was great tribulation for Israel in AD 70. There has been recurring tribulation for the church throughout history. But there will yet come a time of one last major tribulation right before the end.

4. Antichrist will be revealed.

Christ said many false prophets and false messiahs would come (Matt. 24:24). A special one called “the man of sin” is predicted in 2 Thessalonians 2:3–4. Likewise, 1 John 2:18 says there will be one main Antichrist and many lesser antichrists. Some identify this person with the beast of Revelation 13 and other figures. Others say he is not an individual but a system, like the papacy. It would seem that he is the satanic counterpart of Christ, a sort of incarnation of Satan. Much of the world will follow him in his assault on God’s people, but he is doomed to be defeated by Christ at the second coming (Rev. 19:20; 2 Thess. 2:8).

5. Christ will remove Christians from the world.

Right before He returns to earth, Jesus will take living Christians to Heaven without dying, like Enoch and Elijah. We call this the Rapture (see 1 Thess. 4:17; 1 Cor. 15:51; John 14:3; Matt. 24:31). It is an instantaneous transformation and glorification (1 Cor. 15:52; Phil. 3:20). Some think this will happen seven years before Christ returns (i.e., before a future seven-year tribulation), but that would mean two second comings. Christ does this immediately before He comes.

6. Dead Christians will be raised from the dead.

Moments before He takes living Christians from the earth, Christ will raise up all dead believers, including Old Testament believers (1 Cor. 15:51–52; 1 Thess. 4:15–17). They receive new bodies that are perfect, immortal, and without sin. Their resurrection and the rapture of living saints both happen in a split second. Just as angels assist in our deaths, so they will assist in this great event as they announce His coming and come with Him (1 Thess. 4:16; 2 Thess. 1:7). No Christian will be left out, regardless of whether he was buried, cremated, or eaten by lions. We will enter eternity with those new bodies. We will not marry or procreate nor feel pain or death in them (Matt. 22:30; Rev. 21:4). They will be like the perfect body in which the Lord Jesus was raised (Phil. 3:20). This is described in 1 Corinthians 15.

7. Christ will rule on earth for one thousand years.

Revelation 20 is the classic place in the Bible on the thousand-year reign of Christ, or the *millennium*. Some Christians think this period is symbolic of all church history (what is called *amillennialism*). Others think it refers to the golden age of revival at the end of church history (what is known as *postmillennialism*). My view is that the time period of Revelation 20 follows the second coming of Christ in chapter 19 (what is known as *premillennialism*). Christ returns, defeats His enemies, reigns personally with His people for one thousand years, then defeats an enemy uprising, followed by the resurrection of the lost and the last judgment. The key is the two separate resurrections. The resurrection of Christians (the first resurrection) is explicitly said to be separate from the resurrection of unbelievers (the second resurrection) by one thousand years. Since both are future events, the conclusion is that the interval is also future.

8. Unbelievers will be raised from the dead.

John 5:25, Daniel 12:2, Revelation 20:4–6, and other passages say that all people will be raised up one day, including unbelievers. Those who die in their sins will be taken out of Hades, reunited with their bodies, and stay in those bodies forever in Hell. Their bodies will be different than those of Christians. Their bodies will be corruptible, filled with pain and ugliness, always dying but never ceasing to exist. They used their bodies for sinful pleasure, therefore, it is fitting that they pay for those sins by physical torment. None will be excluded.

9. All will appear before the last judgment.

After the millennium, all people will have been raised and will appear before God (Rev. 20:12–13). Everyone who has ever lived will be there. All history has been recorded and will be replayed as evidence (Rev. 20:12). Believers will be exonerated, not because they are innocent, but because their names are in the Book of Life: elected, redeemed, saved (Rev. 20:15; Luke 10:20). They will receive extra rewards according to how they served Christ (2 Cor. 5:10). Unbelievers, however, will be damned (Matt. 25:41–46). Their names are not in the Book of Life (Rev. 13:8; 17:8; 20:15). They have no excuse or escape, no second chance or higher appeal. Before they are executed, they will be forced to bow before the Lord Jesus and confess that He is Lord after all (Phil. 2:10–11). Then they will be sent to Hell forever. The last judgment is predicted over and over in Scripture, such as in Matthew 25 and Revelation 20. Christ will be the Judge, Jury, and Executioner.

10. God will refashion the universe.

Immediately after the last judgment, God will cleanse the universe of the effects of sin. The curse on creation will be lifted (Rev. 22:3). It will be a sort of cosmic resurrection. It is described like a great meltdown in 2 Peter 3, after which it will be remolded into something even greater. Revelation 21 and Isaiah 66 describe it as the "new Heavens and a new earth." Other texts call it the "restoration of all things" (Acts 3:21). It is the last main event in time as such, and the beginning of the eternal state. The glory of God will shine through this creation as never before.

48

The Second Coming

1. Jesus Christ will return to the earth.

The Bible records hundreds of prophecies that Christ will return. Thus, God has promised it over and over. It is absolutely sure and inevitable. Jesus Himself said that He will return (John 14:3). All history awaits this great event, which will be as important to history as Christ's first coming was. We call it the *second coming* as per Hebrews 9:28. Jews who reject Christ as Messiah still await the first coming. The Bible describes this great event as His coming (2 Thess. 2:1); His revelation (1 Peter 1:13); His appearing (Titus 2:13). He will return, descend, invade, and intervene. There will be nothing like it in the history of the world.

2. Christ's second coming will be different from his first coming.

Both comings were predicted by prophets. Both had been foreordained by God. The same Jesus who came will come again (the second coming is not the coming of a second Messiah, like Sun Myung Moon). But there are also big differences. He will not come as a baby, but as an adult. He will not come as a servant, but as a king. He will not come in relative obscurity, but openly for all to behold. He will not come in humility, but in victory. He will not come to die, but to execute and kill. Those who saw the first coming generally saw Him only as a man, but at the next coming we will see Him as the God-man. He came veiled in secrecy; He will return in full glory. It won't be by birth at Bethlehem, but from the sky on a white horse. It will be far greater than we can imagine.

3. Christ has not returned yet.

All sorts of theories have been spun to say that Jesus has already returned. Some say He returned in AD 70 at the destruction of Jerusalem. However, Jude, 1 John, and Revelation were written after AD 70 and looked forward to His return. Others say that Pentecost was the second coming. No, that was the special coming of the Spirit, not of Jesus. Still others say the second coming refers to our conversions or even our deaths. No. In the one, Christ comes into us spiritually, but that is radically different from the second coming. At death, we go to be with Him; He does not come to be with us. Then there are cults who say that Jesus returned invisibly in 1914, 1917, or other dates. But the second coming will be open for all to see (Rev. 1:7).

4. No one knows when Christ will return.

People have been guessing for centuries when Christ will return. They have all been wrong. God simply has not revealed the date, not even information from which we could deduce an approximate date. God alone knows (Mark 13:32). Beware those who think they can add up numbers in the Bible and name the date. It may be centuries away for all we know. Our job is to get the gospel out, not pry into unrevealed secrets (Acts 1:7).

5. There will be only one second coming.

There is a popular but erroneous theory that says there will be more than one second coming. It is called the *pretribulation* rapture theory. It says that Christ will come halfway to earth in a cloud, take us out of earth, then come again all the way to earth seven years later. This would be a second and third coming. But the terms *coming*, *appearing*, *revelation* and *descent* all are interchangeable and refer to the same event. There is no "secret coming" of Christ (Matt. 24:27). The theory is sensational and popular but is not found in the Bible. Christ does several things together at the one second coming, not separately at a second and third coming.

6. Christ will return visibly.

"Every eye will see Him" (Rev. 1:7). Christ compared it to the lightning that is seen from one end of the sky to the other (Matt. 24:27). Believers will see Him and rejoice (1 Peter 4:13). Unbelievers will see and recoil in terror. They will plead for the mountains to fall on them (Rev. 6:16–17). He will return with the blast of a trumpet and shout of an angel (1 Thess. 4:16). That will be loud enough to wake the dead. It will be seen and heard and felt by all. It is open and plain, not secret. He will appear in blazing fire and glorious splendor (2 Thess. 1:7–8).

7. Christ will come with angels and saints.

Christ will not be alone when He comes. He will come with millions of angels (2 Thess. 1:7; Jude 14). He will be accompanied by a heavenly entourage of archangels, seraphim, cherubim, guardian angels, principalities, and powers, all with swords drawn and following His lead. Christ will also be accompanied by His people. He will bring with Him the souls of those saints who have already died and will reunite their souls with their bodies as He comes. He will then take all living Christians to be with Him in the descent from the sky in a cloud. Altogether, there will be millions and millions, all aglow with the glory of God. But it is the Lord Jesus who is the center and focal point of it all.

8. Christ will defeat His enemies.

One of the major reasons for the second coming is to defeat all ungodly enemies of God. He will slay all unbelievers with the sword of His mouth (Rev. 19:21). He will be ablaze in flaming fire that will go forth like a flame-thrower (2 Thess. 1:8). None will escape. He will come to begin the work of judgment on them for their sins. They will know for sure that He is Lord and King. But it will be too late for salvation. Christ will also execute judgment on the False Prophet, the Beast (the Antichrist), and Satan at this time (Rev. 19:20). They will be thrown alive into the lake of fire. Satan will not be able to resist but will crumble like a cobweb under a tank. Christ will come in overwhelming power and victory.

9. Christ will rescue and vindicate His people.

Christ will rescue His people who have been persecuted. He will snatch them away from the clutches of the Antichrist. He will also vindicate them and show that they were right after all. See 2 Thessalonians 1. He will rescue us from death, pain, and especially sin. It will be the culmination of His wonderful work of redemption for us. That is why the Bible calls it the "blessed hope" (Titus 2:13). Every Christian longs to be alive to witness this. But whether we die first or remain alive, we will both witness and experience it. We will be on the winning side.

10. Christ will appear in glory.

Christ is already filled with glory. But that is mainly hidden from us now. At the second coming, the curtains will be pulled back and the wrappers will be taken off to show what is already there (Rev. 6:14). It will be the greatest of all revelations, revealing the splendor of the glory of God as nothing else in history or creation ever has. It will be the direct and full glory of God. Christ is the living conduit of the glory of God, like a prism. The glory will be let loose like the waters flowing from a broken dam. Sinners will shudder in terror, while saints will marvel in holy awe (2 Thess. 1:10). The curtain between Heaven and earth, between the natural and the supernatural, will be pulled back. He will shine in the radiance of His internal pure glory as on the Mount of Transfiguration. It is His by right.

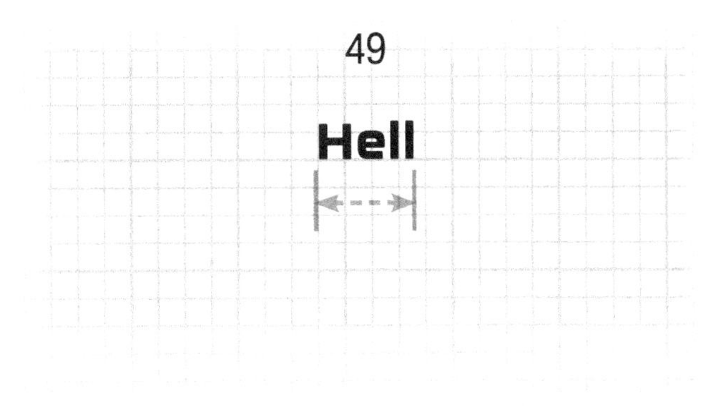

1. Hell is a real place.

The Bible repeatedly speaks about Hell. It is real. It is not a figment of our imaginations, the invention of capitalists to enslave their workers, a make-believe place to scare little children. It was created by God Himself (Matt. 25:41; Isa. 30:33). It is no myth. We are not told exactly where it is located (inside the earth, inside the sun, a black hole, somewhere outside the universe, etc.). It is called by several names in Scripture: Gehenna (Matt. 5:22), outer darkness (Matt. 25:30), the lake of fire (Rev. 20:15), the bottomless pit (Rev. 20:1). It is a place of literal fire where people go in literal physical bodies to be punished. It has fire and brimstone (sulfur) in large supply, so it is a fire that will never go out. Hell is no joke.

2. Satan and demons will be thrown into Hell.

Some fallen angels have been kept in chains in a part of Hades called Tartarus (2 Peter 2:4). One day, they will be transferred to the final Hell. Other demons have been roaming around earth in dread of the day when they too will be consigned to eternal Hell (Matt. 8:29). And Satan himself will be bound and gagged and thrown into the lake of fire (Rev. 19:20; 20:10). Hell was originally created for these evil angelic beings (Matt. 25:41).

3. All unrepentant sinners will go to Hell.

At the last judgment, God will take lost sinners out of Hades, where they have been waiting in torment, and reunite them with their bodies (Rev. 20:5, 13). They will then be judged, condemned, and sent straight to Hell. There will be no exceptions. No unbeliever will somehow sneak into Heaven. Nor will any true Christian be sent to Hell. Of course, no one will want to go there when they see it for what it is. People joke about it now, but they won't then. They will be filled with total terror as they view it in all its horrors. They will be dragged kicking and screaming by angels to be thrown alive into this fiery furnace. It is worse than being thrown alive into a raging volcano. But all their resistance will be futile, and they will wilt like melted butter.

4. Sinners will be punished in Hell.

Hell is the place where God punishes sin and unrepentant sinners. Everyone is a sinner and deserves to go there. Those who go there will have no excuses or appeals (Matt. 7:21–22). They will know that they are getting exactly what they deserve. Hell is not a penitentiary or reformatory. It is not meant to do them good. It is meant to punish them by inflicting intense and eternal pain. It is not purgatory. It is a place of absolute justice. They will be legally punished for their crimes.

5. Sinners suffer in Hell.

Those in Hell are wide awake and conscious. They wish they could die or sleep, but there is no rest there (Rev. 9:6; 14:11). There is only pain and torment. They will suffer all the physical pains imaginable. Every nerve ending in their bodies will be used as a conduit of pain. They will thirst, but there is no water, only molten lava. They will suffer spiritually, mentally, and emotionally. There is not even the comfort from others in Hell, for all become enemies of everyone else. They will be punished by God Almighty Himself. They will be tormented there (Rev. 14:10–11). This is not sadistic torture or cruelty. It is just and right punishment. The least pains in Hell will far exceed the worst pains back on earth.

6. Sinners do not cease to exist in Hell.

There is an erroneous theory that says that Hell is temporary—as soon as someone is thrown in there, he ceases to exist. Eventually, Hell itself will cease to exist. But that is not what the Bible says. They are not annihilated into oblivion there. They keep on living and suffering (Mark 9:42–48). They will wish they could cease to exist, but divine justice will not allow them to escape their punishment. The Antichrist will survive one thousand years in Hell and will not cease to exist (Rev. 20:7). Hell is not a kind of purgatory, in which people suffer only so long and then be annihilated (if they are cleansed or if their sins have been paid for, why not let them out?). They will live there forever.

7. There are degrees of punishment in Hell.

Just as there are degrees of rewards in Heaven, so there are degrees of punishments in Hell (Luke 12:47–48). Those who never heard the gospel will be punished for their sins against natural revelation. Those who heard but disbelieved will be punished worse. Those who only pretended to believe will be punished still worse, then the false prophets and preachers, then Judas, and then Satan worst of all. Those with more sins will receive more punishment and some sins deserve more punishment than others. But even the lightest punishment is extremely intense. As Jonathan Edwards said, those in Hell would give the whole world if they could only reduce the number of their sins by even one. But they can't.

8. There is no mercy in Hell.

On earth, God shows some mercy and some wrath. His wrath is held in check by His common grace. But this is not so in Hell. There is no mercy whatsoever in Hell. There is nothing to hold back the full fury of the wrath of God in Hell. It is where God lets loose His infinite holy anger against sinners who have offended Him by their willful rebellion. His wrath is poured out "unmixed" and pure, without even a drop of mercy (Rev. 14:10). Earth is the closest that these sinners will ever get to Heaven and mercy.

9. Hell is eternal.

Hell is as eternal and everlasting as Heaven (Matt. 25:46). It never ends. Its fire is unquenchable (Mark 9:44, 46, 48). God's wrath is infinite and therefore will never be shut off or satisfied. God will not change His mind. Each sin deserves eternal punishment because it is committed against an infinitely holy God. People are punished infinitely in Hell—not in intensity (there are degrees of intensity) but in duration. Eternity is infinite time. The smoke of Hell goes up forever and ever (Rev. 14:11). Moreover, sinners continue to sin in Hell, not in sin's expression but in its evil state (totally depraved unregenerate sinners can only sin permanently). Therefore, they will add still more fuel to the fires. There will be no escape, no respite, no "time out," no end. It goes on forever.

10. God is glorified in Hell.

God is glorified in the display of His attributes in Hell.

He shows His truth (His warnings were true), His holiness (His will was disobeyed), and even indirectly in His spurned common grace. His overwhelming power will be displayed. But it is especially His wrath that is shown there. Sinners will be separated from God's presence of love but will be tormented in the presence of His holy wrath (Rev. 14:10). God will not receive pleasure from this, but He will receive glory. He will reveal the glory of His wrath, which will be echoed back to Him in the groans of those who are being rightly punished. Those who deny Hell's existence thus defy God and are going there. But no one in Hell has any doubts about Hell—or the wrath of God.

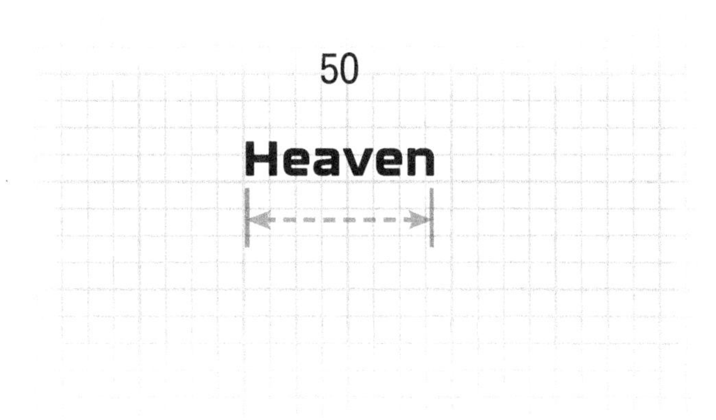

50 Heaven

1. Heaven is our eternal home.

Heaven is real. It is not wishful thinking, a never-never land of childish dreams. In fact, Heaven is more real than earth. Heaven is the eternal destiny and final resting place of all true Christians. It is sometimes described as a home (2 Cor. 5:5). It is home sweet home. There's no place like this home. We will be gathered together with the rest of our spiritual family, to live forever in our Father's home. We belong there because we are in the family. See John 14:2.

2. There is no pain in Heaven.

There will be no physical, mental, or emotional pain in Heaven (Rev. 21:4). There will be no sorrow or tears there. There will be no regrets. Nobody will miss earth. There will be no sad memories. There will be no worries. There will be no fatigue or fear, or any other negative emotion. All pain is in Hell, where there is no pleasure. Also, there will be no death in Heaven—only eternal life.

3. There is full pleasure in Heaven.

Heaven is the place of exquisite pleasures of all sorts. There will be perfect peace there. There will be overflowing joy. There will be rest from all tiring labor (Rev. 14:13). Even work in Heaven will be pleasurable. The internal spiritual pleasures will far outweigh the external physical pleasures of Heaven, great as they may be. "In Your presence is fullness of joy, at Your right hand are pleasures forevermore" (Ps. 16:11). Earth is mixed with pain and pleasure. Earth is the closest that we will ever get to Hell. Pain will be only a distant memory in Heaven and even that memory will not cause pain. It is irreligious to ask if there will be pleasurable things like baseball in Heaven. God Himself will be the source of Heaven's pleasure. We will truly enjoy God to the fullest, even to overflowing. It is pure and perfect joy.

4. Heaven is a place of holiness.

There is no sin in Heaven (Rev. 21:8, 27). That alone would make it a wonderful place. All sin is left outside. Christians are made sinless, not only legally but experientially (Eph. 1:4; 5:27; Rev. 20:6; 22:11). There will never be a "fall number two." We will be made holy and pure and impeccable. The holiness of God will be revealed there and will transform everything and everyone there into living conduits of His holiness. Heaven is alive and pulsating with holiness.

5. We will receive rewards in Heaven.

Just as there are degrees of punishment in Hell, so there are degrees of rewards in Heaven (Matt. 25:14–23). This does not include salvation, which is by grace alone. But Christ will give rewards to all of us according to how we obeyed on earth. They will be gauged by factors such as how much we sacrificed, how much we suffered, how we followed the will of the Lord as we knew it, etc. Some will have more than others (apostles, prophets, martyrs, missionaries, etc.). Some will have few because they lived only a short time after their conversions, like the dying thief. Others will receive large rewards because they were converted young and lived a long life of faithful service. But those with fewest will not envy those with more, for all are perfectly happy.

6. We will meet other Christians.

We will meet the rest of the family, from Adam onwards (Matt. 8:11). We will meet Old Testament believers, New Testament saints, great Christians from church history. We will be reunited with dear relatives and friends. We will meet those who witnessed to us briefly and never saw us again. We will meet our converted spouses, though we will not be married to them anymore (Matt. 22:30). We will recognize each other, even in our perfected bodies. We will share happy memories and testimonies of God's grace. We will see all those in Heaven, including the holy angels. But we will also be able to view those in Hell (Luke 16:22–24). This will not frighten or worry us, however. Rather, it will cause us to thank God for saving us and to glorify God as He righteously punishes them. See Revelation 19:1–4 and Psalm 91:8.

7. Christ and His bride will be united in heavenly marriage.

We were betrothed in election and engaged in conversion. One day the greatest of all marriages will happen (Rev. 19:7; 21:2). Each of us will be married to Christ and enjoy a full and perfect union with Him. But the bride also consists of all true Christians, so this union will be between all them and us and with our beloved Jesus. It is spiritual, not physical. Sex will not be physical. The union will be far greater. It will produce a progeny of glory and bliss and eternal love. It will, of course, be permanent and indissoluble. We will know Christ deeper and deeper into all eternity.

8. We will see God.

God is presently invisible and hidden. In Heaven, He will reveal Himself visibly to us. We will see Him with our very eyes. This is called the *beatific vision*. See Matthew 5:8; 1 Corinthians 13:12; 1 John 3:2. "They shall see His face" (Rev. 22:4). We will also see God spiritually and mentally. We will understand more of what He had not revealed and will understand more and more into all eternity but will never understand everything about God. We will gaze upon our precious Savior in all His beauty and grace and glory (Ps. 27:4; Isa. 33:17). We will look at God looking at us, eye to eye, heart to heart, with nothing to block the vision. And we will see God forever and ever.

9. We will love and be loved by God forever.

God elected us so as to show us the glory of His grace (Eph. 1:4–6; 2:7). We will receive this love in Heaven. Heaven is a world of love, an ocean without shore or bottom, in which we will swim and bathe forever. Romans 9:23 says that God elected and saved us so that we would become vessels of mercy—containers of His love and goodness and grace. He will fill us to overflowing and increase our capacity so we may receive more. In turn, we will love Him for first loving us. He will never stop loving us and we will never stop loving Him.

10. God's glory will be revealed.

The ultimate purpose for which God created all things is to display His glory (Rom. 11:36). He does this at last in Heaven (in Hell in another way). He will reveal the beauty of His glory in all its splendor and radiance, transforming everything and everyone there into living mirrors that reflect glory to everyone else and back to God. He will reveal the glory of all He is in His many attributes, like bright light in all its wondrous colors. We will be overwhelmed in awe. We will respond in love, humility, and worship. We will adore God forever. His being and glory are infinite, so He will be increasingly revealed forever and ever. And thus will be fulfilled God's plan of the ages.

Recommended Reading

Introductory

Boice, James Montgomery. *Foundations of the Christian Faith*. Downers Grove, IL: InterVarsity Press, 1992.

Frame, John M. *Salvation Belongs to the Lord*. Phillipsburg, NJ: P & R, 2006.

Grudem, Wayne. *Christian Beliefs*. Grand Rapids: Zondervan, 2005.

House, H. Wayne. *Charts of Systematic Theology*. Grand Rapids: Zondervan, 2006.

Lloyd-Jones, D. Martyn. *Great Doctrines of the Bible*. Wheaton, IL: Crossway Books, 1996.

Packer, J. I. *Concise Theology*. Wheaton, IL: Tyndale House, 1996.

——— *Knowing Christianity*. Wheaton, IL: Harold Shaw, 1995.

Sproul, R. C. *Essential Truths of the Christian Faith*. Wheaton, IL: Tyndale, 1992.

Advanced

à Brakel, Wilhelmus. *The Christian's Reasonable Service*. Ligonier, PA: Soli Deo Gloria, 1992.

Beeke, Joel R., and Paul M. Smalley. *Reformed Systematic Theology*. Grand Rapids: Reformation Heritage Books, 2019.

Berkhof, Louis. *Systematic Theology*. Grand Rapids: Eerdmans, 1988.

Boyce, James Petigru. *Abstract of Systematic Theology*. Cape Coral, FL: Founders, 2006.

Culver, Robert. *Systematic Theology*. Fearn: Christian Focus, 2005.

Erickson, Millard. *Christian Theology*. Grand Rapids: Baker Book House, 1993.

Grudem, Wayne. *Systematic Theology*. Grand Rapids: Zondervan, 1994.

Hodge, Charles. *Systematic Theology*. Grand Rapids: Eerdmans, 1979.

Letham, Robert. *Systematic Theology*. Wheaton, IL: Crossway, 2019.

MacArthur, John, and Richard Mayhue, eds. *Biblical Doctrines*. Wheaton, IL: Crossway, 2017.

Shedd, William G. T. *Dogmatic Theology*. Phillipsburg, NJ: P & R, 2003.

Reference Works

Cairns, Alan. *Dictionary of Theological Terms*. Greenville, SC: Ambassador Emerald International, 2002.

Davie, Martin, Tim Grass, Stephen R. Holmes, John McDowell, and T. A. Noble, eds. *New Dictionary of Theology*. 3rd ed. Downers Grove, IL: InterVarsity Press, 2016.

Elwell, Walter, ed. *Topical Analysis of the Bible*. Grand Rapids: Baker Book House, 1991.

Erickson, Millard. *Concise Dictionary of Christian Theology*. Grand Rapids: Baker Book House, 1986.

Treier, Daniel J., and Walter A. Elwell, eds. *Evangelical Dictionary of Theology*. 3rd ed. Grand Rapids: Baker Academic, 2017.

The Failure of Natural Theology: A Critical Appraisal of the Philosophical Theology of Thomas Aquinas

Jeffrey D. Johnson

Johnson's scholarly but gracefully readable text shows that his intellect notwithstanding, Aquinas's mingled metaphysics, mixed methodology, and promotion of "divine immobility" merit strong caution. This is the book the church has needed on this subject. It is an urgent read by one of our best theologians.

—Dr. Owen Strachan

The Missionary Crisis: Five Dangers Plaguing Missions and How the Church Can Be the Solution

Paul Snider

The Missionary Crisis confronts five dangers facing missionaries and the local churches that send them and gives biblical and practical instruction for missionaries, sending churches, and mission organizations. This book boldly approaches gentle correction for the missionary to reverse these five crises in their ministries. It challenges the local church to prepare and equip men and women for the high calling of missionary life.

Seven Thoughts Every Christian Ought to Think Every Day: Laying a Foundation for a Life of Prayer

Jim Scott Orrick

Searching for great resources to disciple new believers can be like Goldilocks tasting porridge. Too difficult, and it frustrates; too fluffy, and it misleads. Jim Orrick has that much sought-after gift of taking deep truths and bringing the tray to the common man. When a book can be handed to an unbeliever for evangelism, read through with a new believer to disciple, worked through with the family for worship, and also delight the soul of the seasoned in Christ, it is a helpful book.

– Josh Lagrange, Church planter

The Gospel Made Clear to Children

Jennifer Adams

The highest recommendation I can give to this wonderful book is that I will be reading it over and over again to my children. It is rich in biblical doctrine and is an invaluable instrument to aid parents in teaching their children the glorious truths of "God in Christ" reconciling the world to Himself. I know of no other book that so clearly communicates the great doctrines of the gospel to children.

– Paul Washer,
Author, Director of HeartCry Missionary Society

Ten Essential Sermons of Charles Spurgeon

Introduction by Tom J. Nettles

I like to read Spurgeon because his fierce passion for biblical truth comes through so clearly, even in print. I greatly admire his commitment to sound doctrine, his hatred of heresy, his passion for souls, and his knowledge of Scripture. But more than anything else, I appreciate his deep love for Christ. All of it is contagious.

– John MacArthur

Visit
www.freegracepress.com
for these and many
other excellent resources.